Indiana
Ghost
Folklore

Tom Baker

Schiffer
Publishing Ltd

4880 Lower Valley Road, Atglen, Pennsylvania 19310

Schiffer Books are available at special discounts for bulk purchases for sales promotions or premiums. Special editions, including personalized covers, corporate imprints, and excerpts can be created in large quantities for special needs. For more information contact the publisher:

Schiffer Publishing Ltd.
4880 Lower Valley Road
Atglen, PA 19310
Phone: (610) 593-1777; Fax: (610) 593-2002
E-mail: Info@schifferbooks.com

For the largest selection of fine reference books on this and related subjects, please visit our web site at **www.schifferbooks.com** We are always looking for people to write books on new and related subjects. If you have an idea for a book please contact us at the above address.

This book may be purchased from the publisher. Include $5.00 for shipping. Please try your bookstore first. You may write for a free catalog.

In Europe, Schiffer books are distributed by
Bushwood Books
6 Marksbury Ave.
Kew Gardens
Surrey TW9 4JF England
Phone: 44 (0) 20 8392-8585; Fax: 44 (0) 20 8392-9876
E-mail: info@bushwoodbooks.co.uk
Website: www.bushwoodbooks.co.uk

Designed by Stephanie Daugherty
Type set in Impact Regular/New Baskerville BT

ISBN: 978-0-7643-3334-7
Printed in The United States of America

Contents

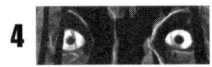

Dedication

This book is dedicated to my entire family, most especially Terri Lynn Juarez, my wonderful grandparents, Bill and Rosemary Everman, my mother, Brenda Durham, my father, Sergeant David Baker, and to friends who have remained loyal over the years: Abe Sandoval, Jason Leonard, and Matt Losure. Thank you for being a few lights in an often darkening world. It is also dedicated to those who have already passed on "into that good night." We will meet again, someday.

Acknowledgments

Special acknowledgements should be given the staff of the Marion Public Library for their invaluable assistance and tolerance, the staff of the Waldenbooks at the North Park Mall in Marion, Indiana, for their kindness and support, and the staff of the *Chronicle Tribune* of Marion, Indiana, for their invaluable support. It is the presence of people such as these that make life worth living.

Is all that we see, or seem,
But a dream within a dream?

~Edgar Allen Poe

Foreword

The woman sat clutching her heaving chest, breathing heavily in the darkness. She had seen it all clearly: the boy, bobbing up and down in the water like some sort of doomed apple, surfacing for air, before being drawn back down, as if by malicious, invisible hands, to his untimely death. She knew, with a creeping horror of certainty, that what she had just witnessed was, in fact, a future event; a vision of something that had not yet occurred but was so fated and ordered by whatever logic controlled the seemingly otherwise random happenings of the world.

At breakfast she told her husband, "Don't tell Chet, but I had a dream that Lemoines Lee drowned last night."

The woman (who was known, at times, to have such prognostications and dreams), was duly troubled. How much more troubled could she have been then when, upon her son Chet waking up (he had been home sick from school all week) and sitting down to lunch, a neighbor stopped by to inform them of some grave news...Lemoines Lee had gone to the swimming hole at lunchtime—he had drowned.

It is an old-fashioned story of psychic foresight, and it is the sort of story that the pages of the present volume are chiefly concerned with. We have assembled a plethora of stories, each skirting the boundary between fact and fancy, folklore and phenomenon, the real and the powerfully unreal, to bring to you a hint of that netherworld that exists between the spaces known and unknown. For our setting, we have the otherwise placid, nondescript background of the Hoosier state, Indiana, a place so eerily normal and "run-of-the-mill," you just know, at a deeply internal level, that it must be crawling with dark and sinister things.

If, as the great chronicler of unexplained phenomenon Charles Fort once said, "you can measure a circle beginning anywhere," then we have certainly followed through with this philosophy in the organization and structure of our little book, as we present to you, willy-nilly, a potpourri of paranormal delights, both sinister and surprising, and heap them up until you either succumb to incredulity, or pronounce yourself a "true believer." Whether you do or don't is all the same to us, but we promise you the danger of losing your skepticism (or not) is hidden within these powerful pages.

The preceding anecdote was from the history of my own family. Here's another such anecdote. My grandmother once had a dream, when her own mother was getting quite old, of sitting at a family dinner. There was an old-time Victrola turning a record in the background. Suddenly, in the disembodied fashion of dreams, she could see the record turning

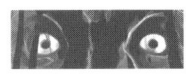
on the player. It was an old gospel song, popular in its day. It was called: "Tell Mother I'll Be Waiting There."

It must have been very popular at funerals.

It was only a short time later that her mother did, indeed, pass away, and my grandmother has always connected the dream with that event. Whatever connection actually exists is a matter of debate, but one thing is for certain: These experiences do happen to average people, and have been since the beginning of man's ascent. They should not be taken lightly.

One day, we shall all take that *Final Journey*, and perhaps we shall know the answer concerning where the "There" mentioned in the old gospel song exactly is, or if it is at all. Until then, all we have are anecdotes, experiences, and tales. Lots and lots of them.

1

Hey, Want to Go For a Ride?

T he sweeping fields of rural Indiana are crowned, on genuinely nice days, by an often cloud-bestrewn expanse of deep blue sky that seems to roll on just about forever. On such days, while actively walking through the high grasses of the fields surrounding my home and letting the little dog I had at the time lead me forward, I would often ruminate on a subject that has come to mean very much to me, over the years.

That subject is, quite simply, the subject of Unidentified Flying Objects, or, as more popularly known, "UFOs."

It is certainly one of the strangest areas of folklore ever to emerge from the human experience. Going back thousands of years, into the misty fog of antiquity, UFO events are even recorded in the Holy Bible in several accounts, including the mysterious (and oft repeated) experience of Ezekiel, who delivered an electrifying account of a glowing "wheel within a wheel" emerging over a river and the mysterious "living creatures" which inhabited it. Of course, likewise, Moses led the Children of Israel out of bondage in Egypt while following a "pillar of cloud by day" and a "pillar of fire by night."

Down through the ages, UFOs have always been a subterranean undercurrent of knowledge and experience, one that promised fascination and danger to any who dared seek out the truth behind this enigmatic aerial caper. The ancient Greeks had a special office of inquiry just for UFOs, and they continued to be sighted intermittently throughout Medieval and into modern Western history.

Many researchers, most notably the Swiss theorist Erich Von Daniken, suppose the strange aerial visitors had an enormous hand in helping primitive peoples build the mysterious monuments of their vanished civilizations, such as the Great Pyramid of Giza and the strange ground markings on the Nazca Plateau in Peru.

Whether or not any of this conjecture has any relation to solid fact is a matter of personal decision and faith, but one thing that certainly cannot be denied, no matter an individual's personal schema of belief, is that the phenomenon of unidentified aerial sightings and reported "strange visitations" has had as great an impact on our society and way of thought as has any supposition which has come before it. The U.S. government has sponsored several official investigations (the last one, *Project Blue Book*, was officially ended in 1969), and for over half a century, an entire industry has grown up in the wake of the first American UFO scare in 1947: Films, books, television programs, games, comic books, music, clothing, memorabilia, and urban legends abound concerning the possibility of intelligent life existing "elsewhere," and an entire controversial field of research, *Ufology*, has risen (some might say badly) to the challenge of confronting this lingering mystery.

And as if speculations concerning mysterious happenings in the sky were not enough, beginning in the middle sixties, with the famous case of Betty and Barney Hill, and growing into a veritable cult-like religion throughout the eighties and nineties, multitudes of people began to come forward, some quite credibly, to report that they had been "abducted" aboard UFOs, given bizarre medical examinations, and then released, often after being shown alien-human hybrid fetuses (and in some reports, living children) and often having their memories, somehow, "erased." Many of these accounts come from people who have undergone the controversial techniques associated with regressive hypnosis.

Indeed, this second aspect of Ufology has taken on a life all its own, with a cadre of researchers, experiencers, support groups, and an entire philosophical *weltanschauung* dedicated to unraveling the mystery of why, exactly, the aliens are here and to what ends are they carrying on their alleged "genetic experiment,"—with the general consensus being that they are here to preserve humanity as a species, just in case we manage to annihilate ourselves off the surface of the planet.

Of course, the great State of Indiana has its fair share of UFO sightings, and, not surprisingly so, since the state is rife with wide-open flat fields, and the aforementioned vast expanses of sky. To sojourn through the Indiana countryside at night can be a lonely, alienating experience, but, if one is looking for UFOs, it can quickly become a journey into the heart of the surreal.

However, one doesn't have to go out in the country to experience a UFO event. There are innumerable instances of folks in the small towns and cities that have turned a corner at the right place and time, and suddenly found themselves subjected with a glimmering starburst from the land of the unknown.

One such story recounts a young girl who was making her sleepy way up to bed one evening, trudging up the stairs. Her way took her past a window that looked out on an expansive backyard, at the edge of which was an old tree, its bare branches sticking outward like greedy fingers above the soft, crunchy mound of autumn leaves that gathered at the base of its trunk.

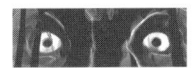

She suddenly noted that a beam of light seemed to trail across the window. At first, she thought it might be from an airplane, or perhaps even the reflection from a passing automobile. She then stopped at the window, looking out, and froze with sheer terrible wonder.

There was a bright, glowing, *something* floating just above treetop outside, hovering over the backyard. The girl felt her mouth fall open, and her heart began to race. Her mind told her that there was no conventional explanation for the large, glowing, floating object that was lighting up the expanse of her backyard—even as she stood there, stock-still and frozen like a doe in the oncoming rush of traffic.

Then, just as suddenly as it had come, the object began to lift upward, silently, and suddenly shot nearly straight upward, at a terrific speed. The girl suddenly broke from the spell of the unearthly weirdness, pressed her face to the glass, straining to see the thing as it went on its way. Of course, all she could see now was a glowing pinpoint of light that had, faintly, the semblance of a glowing star.

Whatever it had been, no one really believed her when she dared bring the subject up, and her mother put it down to "nervous imaginings." This author was told the story first hand many years after it occurred.

Of course, it is not the most fantastic UFO event in Indiana history. A much more unsettling event happened to an unsuspecting carload of teenagers, making their way back home from a church social.

It was while rounding a corner in the middle of town that the car radio suddenly began to go fuzzy, and the engine sputtered out. The car came to a slow roll as the driver muttered an oath to himself.

Suddenly, one of the girls in the back seat happened to look up, and said, excitedly, "What in the world is that?"

The passengers looked out of the windows, peering above them, and not quite being able to believe what it was they were seeing.

It was a circular, dark object floating, noiselessly, directly overhead. Around the rim, there was a number of alternating blinking lights. The object appeared, for the entire world, to be a classic flying saucer.

Suddenly, a beam of light came down, creating a canopy of illumination overhead. Someone in the car began to complain of a high, ringing noise.

Then, just as instantly as it had come, the strange, saucer-like object shot away at an incredible speed, seeming almost to "blink out" in the distance. The car suddenly came rumbling back to life, and the radio began to function properly again.

By the time the group of young people got home, many of them complained of feeling nausea and headache, and those who had looked directly at the light streaming down from the strange craft felt their eyes itch and burn. Their parents did not believe them, despite their protestations that what they had seen had been real. Later, several of the teens were afflicted with strange dreams, and none of them ever forgot their singular experience.

Of course, one does not have to go out for a drive in the country to experience UFOs. According to witnesses, the phenomenon can happen anywhere, at anytime. Abductees report experiencing UFO abductions in the middle of the night, while sleeping in their beds, by beings that can seemingly enter and leave through solid walls.

One of the strangest cases of a Hoosier UFO encounter this author has ever had the privilege of knowing was that of a young man and his aunt, who enjoyed the pleasure of walking with each other at night. This may seem strange to contemporary readers, but even as late as fifteen years ago, the crime problem that plagues us currently was not quite as extraordinary as the deterioration of current society has apparently made it. At any rate, the duo felt absolutely no compunction about taking a walk for exercise around the surrounding neighborhoods of an apartment complex at night. Together, they felt reasonably safe.

To begin with, it should be stressed to the reader that the location of the apartment complex was situated between a few rolling yards, bordered on one side by steep, residential neighborhoods, and on the other by a former radio station, which abutted an open field and a lighted antenna.

The street went down, intersecting with an avenue on the other side of which lay a sprawling factory complex with large parking lots on either side. Beyond that were the highway, the cornfields, and the inevitable back roads stretching through farm fields and desolate Hoosier countryside.

The duo had begun walking just after dark, talking amicably, but feeling no particular urgency to be back by any certain time. The young man's mother was waiting for both of them back at the apartment, but she was busily watching television, and so the two had much time to walk and talk.

While going through a nice, well-kept area, the young boy continually talking as they went, they became conscious of a mysterious black van pulling up toward them, slowing down, as a driver leaned out the window.

"Hey, you guys want to go for a ride?"

The duo was immediately cautious.

"No thanks, man," said the boy.

It was dark, so the man looking out the window was little more than a vague silhouette.

The boy and his aunt continued walking, slowly, down the sidewalk in front of the quiet houses, occasionally whispering between themselves until they were certain that the black van that had pulled up had driven away.

"Okay, those guys were really weird."

"Why would they think we wanted a ride?"

The two continued to walk, making small talk, nervously, as they went. The duo followed the curve of the street until it let out onto a main thoroughfare, and then walked past a nursing home, an old field (which bordered the apartment complex on one side), and proceeded around the corner. Across the street, a massive field abutted a disused radio station. There was an apartment complex on one end, and a row of houses leading down the street toward the other. Neighborhoods and fields intersected, but directly across from them as they walked toward the main entrance of the parking complex was the largest field. The boy caught a glimmer of something out of the corner of his eye, but was so absorbed in his conversation that he paid it no mind. They may have been talking about vacations, or rock bands (Motley Crue was, like, really hot that long-ago year), or they may have still been nervous about that black van. It did not really matter, because neither of them could remember what on earth they had been talking about later during that long, strange walk.

The night was warm, the stars were vivid overhead.

"Hey, what is that?" The aunt asked the boy in a kind of casual nervousness as they both approached the apartment complex sign.

There was no sidewalk here, so they both were leaning a bit at the edge of the road. Finally, they hit the pavement directly in front of the place, and began walking toward the aunt's apartment when the boy looked over, to answer, "It's just a helicopter."

"Uh, it's not making any noise."

The boy suddenly felt prickles on the back of his neck, and they both turned to stare directly across the street at the black field beyond. Hovering, silently, as if watching them like a predator, was a dark, cigar-shaped body with a brilliant light on either end. It was enormous, perhaps the length of three school busses joined end to end, and as it rose, silently, less than 100 feet away from them, a sinister, hypnotizing strobe flashed, lightening-like on top.

The thing arced upward at an enormous rate, so that they finally caught a glimpse of the black underside of the (now unmistakable) UFO. Then, it seemed to explode into a brilliant scarlet flash, and zipped away into the nighttime sky, leaving the two witnesses as stunned and perplexed as if they had been deer caught in the headlights of an oncoming truck.

"What…in the *hell* was that?"

Indeed, the thing was now a fading pinpoint of light among the stars. It had seemed not to so much fly away as *hop* from its hovering position into the distance, among the other pinpoints of light.

"That was…someone who was a little off course. Like a few million light years."

The boy started to laugh at his remark, but they both felt strangely at ease with what they had just seen. Particularly the aunt, who seemed to accept the unknown nature of what she had just witnessed as easily as if it had been a cheap illusion.

We will leave our mystified duo for the time being. One of them will crop up again in the august pages of this fine little book you are now holding eagerly in your hot little hands.

In his book *UFOs: Operation Trojan Horse*, author John Keel (who also wrote the fantastic paranormal classic *The Mothman Prophecies*) postulates that certain geographical locations operate as "windows of opportunity" for weird happenings. Or, to be a bit more esoteric, that that portion of reality that cannot be seen or sensed with the naked eye (as much of the fantastic spectrum of what we think of as reality cannot) can, at the appropriate time, with the appropriate persons present, manifest itself in a variety of bizarre, shocking ways. Mr. Keel (who must, by now, be acknowledged as a veritable Einstein of the unexplained) has done nothing less than offer for us a Universal Field Theory of irrational phenomena, tying the seemingly disparate world of poltergeists, UFOs, hairy creatures, sea monsters, unbelievable coincidences, magic, ESP, witchcraft, Marian apparitions, psychic channeling, clairvoyance, and, of course, ghosts, ghosts (and more ghosts), together for us on a frequency band that can be accessed by some, and involuntarily tuned into by many at the right time, in the right place.

He goes so far as to suggest that this "electromagnetic force" that creates temporary "transmogrifications" of energy and matter in an attempt to communicate with us is outside the scope of linear time; has, hence, been involved in this game since the beginning of recorded history; is all-knowing, all-seeing, and capable of performing miracles and virtually limitless in the scope of what it can accomplish, at least as far as what we know. In addition, that it may be, finally, inconceivable to the human mind.

Feeling a wee bit paranoid yet?

Good. We have started off on our journey on the right foot, or hit the right note, if you prefer. Perhaps you feel a wee bit jittery just thinking about the possibility that you may be living next door (or, heavens forbid, above) one of these yawning psychic crevices, these theoretical whirlpools of weirdness that allow such phantasms of the human mind to seep and creep through, perform absurd miracles (or do other devious things), and then vanish, leaving the respective witnesses to the phenomena as baffled as if they had just been struck by a thunderbolt of Jupiter.

If this all-pervasive force Keel postulates is what we (or most of us, at any rate) think of as God, then perhaps, he suggests, we had better give God a second thought. Keel intimates in *Trojan Horse* a baffling litany of strange occurrences and terrified witnesses, of latter-day mystics channeling "space brothers," and mysterious poltergeists that clutch at their victims while they are sleeping, throw objects to and fro around their domiciles, and hover over them at night

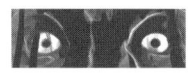

in the form of large, long-fingered phantoms. Much of this phenomena is tied to "window-areas" such as Point Pleasant, West Virginia, areas in Michigan, Wisconsin, (most certainly Texas), and of course, California as well.

We would do well to add the state of Indiana to the list. For we have collected for your delectation and edification a series of baffling occurrences, spectral spooks, haunted hallways, houses that creak (and gibber, and groan), and people that vanish without a seeming trace, and all of these collected tales have one thing in common: They all hail from the seemingly placid, perfectly American state of Indiana, a Window of Opportunity for Things That Should Not Be, if ever there was one.

We have combed the forbidden history of the Hoosier State in search of forgotten little phantoms, of Hairy Whatsits that dine on family dogs, of Slithering Somethings that swim, not beneath a Loch in Scotland, but beneath a lake in Indiana, the eeriest place on Planet Earth.

(And we should know. We have lived almost our entire lives here.)

Together, we'll ride down the primrose pathways of bashful bogeymen, and lurk about the decaying hallways of structures where it is said the dead still roam about in eternal bondage to their former abodes. We'll tiptoe through the folklore of the prairie magicians, the spiritualist prophets, and the downright deranged and we'll see if, truly, He of the Hooked Hand still stalks the darkness of Devil's Hollow.

Our volume will take you on another terror-packed tour of the paranormal realm, and, unlike our previous book *Haunted Indianapolis*, this particular journey will take us far a field of the run-of-the-mill haunts, into a land so mind-bogglingly bizarre it may threaten to leave you, dear reader, shrieking in a nightmare of ecstasy from which few, if any, ever return unchanged.

So settle in. Dim the lights. There's a good fellow. You're all comfy and warm in your chair. Somewhere, not far away, a Window is opening (perhaps beneath your very feet?), and *Something* is trying to get through. To You. It wants to be friends.

It knows you're alone.

It might be a shimmering shade, a knock on the wall, a hairy thing that is neither ape nor man, or a bright glowing vehicle from a world beyond, but, whatever the case, it looks around the area, and it likes what it sees. It feels at home.

Oh, and just you mind to close the curtains as night falls. You never know what you might witness hovering around in the backyard, lurking through the bushes, or peeping in at you as you nod off in your chair. It might be something that would force you to rethink your entire outlook on life, and to reconsider what is real and unreal, possible and impossible, fantasy and nightmare.

Come on. I think our ride is waiting.

Let's go!

2

Oliver Lerch

One of the strangest stories to emerge from the dust-strewn pages of haunted lore is that of a little boy, an enigmatic tot with the unlikely sobriquet of Oliver Lerch. It is a story as fascinating as it is frightening, and one that rings forth with resounding implications for humankind.

Young Oliver was a South Bend farm boy who, one solitary evening, as the sun was beginning to dip below the trees, was asked by his dear mother to go to the well and fetch a bucket of fresh water. We must assume that there was nothing, whatsoever, out of the ordinary about this request, and that young Oliver might have repeated this action numerous times over the span of his young life. Whatever the case, he headed out the back door, took twenty steps toward the well, and disappeared into the gathering gloom.

Minutes ticked away, and, suddenly, as the family was settling down to dinner, the absence of young Oliver became glaringly apparent. The mother must have become irritable; the father might have cast his face up, unknowingly, from his plate and wondered what was keeping his youngest son.

Mrs. Lerch made her way out the screen door, into the warm summer night. The name of young Oliver had been floating on her lips as a call, but, all of a sudden, as she stepped out onto the rickety old porch, the floorboards groaning and wheezing under the weight of her feet, she felt a sudden pang of fear slice at her heart. The boy was nowhere to be seen. She went out into the yard, following his little footprints (the boy went without shoes in the summertime) until they stopped, still quite a considerable distance from the well.

Her first thought had been that he had, perhaps, fallen to his death in the well during some childish misadventure. She was somewhat relieved, at first, to see (even by the fading twilight)

17

that his footprints ended far from it. Then, immediately, the puzzling nature of this struck her dumb—she felt her heart began to race. Then, suddenly:

Mama! Help me! Mama!

The words seemed to ride around her ears like a strange gust of wind.

She called out, loudly, "Oliver! Oliver! Where are you, Oliver?"

Mama! Help me! Mama!

She suddenly went into a panic, flying back into the house, hardly aware of what she was even saying. Soon, her husband, and Oliver's brothers and sisters, were all standing in the yard, calling out the boy's name.

Help me! Help me! Mama!

"Oliver! Oliver! Boy, where are you! Can you hear me?" The father's stern voice shot out in the gathering gloom.

The disembodied voice of young Oliver came back in reply, seeming to come from everywhere and nowhere. The father went back in the house to get a lantern to shine down the mouth of the well, just in case the boy might be there. Even as he did this, though, he realized it was in vain. There was nothing there, of course.

A search party was quickly convened, complete with a few dogs. It all proved to be futile, however. Oliver Lerch was not seen or heard from again, and after a short while, even his voice seemed to fade out like a weakening signal from an old, beaten radio.

The enigmatic footprints pointed to nothing, giving no evidence whatsoever as to what might have been the unfortunate lad's sorry fate. Indeed, the fact that they simply stopped, as if Oliver had been lifted clean from the earth by some invisible force, seemed to suggest possibilities too hideously nightmarish to even entertain.

We might stop to consider, for a brief moment, the possibility that there are (in the words of the late, great occult writer H.P. Lovecraft) "spaces between" our world and the next, bizarre cracks in the fabric of our dimensional reality that, like fissures upon some metaphysical fault-line, open momentarily. These yawning "Mouths of Hell" might be perfectly invisible, and, indeed, threaten no one as long as no one is unfortunate enough to be in their immediate vicinity while they are opening.

These invisible portals might lead (like the rabbit hole in *Alice in Wonderland*) to a

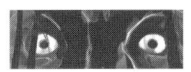

world far stranger and more surreal than anything we can imagine; or, they may lead to a virtual limbo, a nowhere place of cold nothingness, like a cavernous black canyon in the fabric of space and time where what enters can find no hope of leaving ever again. Perhaps young Oliver was sucked into such a supernatural vortices, and died there.

Or, even more troubling, perhaps he is there still.

Time may pass differently in such far-off dimensions.

There is still so much we, as human beings, can never know.

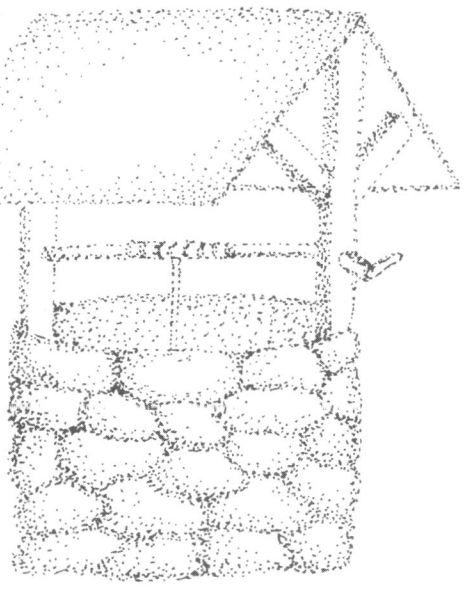

In an interesting side-note, the bizarre tale of the disappearing Southbend farm boy bears a striking resemblance to an even older, more obscure case, that of "Orion Williamson," a man that disappeared, in full view of witnesses, while walking across his own yard one sunny morning. Like the case of young Oliver, the family of Orion Williamson called his name in a futile attempt to communicate with him and find out whither he was whisked to, so suddenly. He, like young Oliver, was never seen again, and his disembodied voice finally faded into silence.

In an ironic twist, that seemingly true occurrence inspired the curmudgeonly horror writer Ambrose Bierce to write his classic short novel "The Damned Thing," which wove a tale of an invisible predator from another dimension that ravaged its prey. One hopes that Oliver Lerch never met such a predator on his surreal, final sojourn.

Bierce, interestingly, also disappeared at the end of his life, while visiting Mexico. He vanished without a trace.

3

Aesop Wilson's Ghost

The story of Aesop Wilson is one that is both poignant and disturbing in equal measure.

Imagine, if you will, a time when the body of a young man that had, prematurely, met his fate could be kept in a casket at the top of the stairs of an old house, with no one thinking very much about it. Here lies the central subject of this very strange vignette.

Dr. Creed Taylor Wilson had come to Indiana to build a house that he, literally, had envisioned only in a dream. He laid the foundations of his home in Medora, where he hoped to set down roots and rear a family of which he could be proud. His wife, a devoted mother to her young son, was overjoyed at the move, and finally felt that the family move to this new, untrammeled territory was a chance to lay down the sorts of roots that stretch onward, into the future, for generations.

The year of the move was 1848. The future of the country would soon be rocked by the bloody epoch of the Civil War, a catastrophic conflagration that would grab the best and hardiest of young Americans in its bloody embrace, sweeping them to an early, violent grave. Unfortunately for the Wilson family, they would not be spared the tragedy of this blistering episode in American history, as their young son, Aesop, was called into service. He quickly dispatched to a camp in Missouri, where he was a part of Indiana Volunteer Company B, 22nd Regiment. Unfortunately, perhaps, he was denied the consolation of a hero's death on the battlefield, contracting typhoid quite early in his service.

His body was shipped back to his family, where a grieving mother seemed to become psychologically unhinged at the reality of losing her young son. She demanded the preservation of young Aesop's body in a lead coffin, which she likewise had placed in an upstairs hallway.

It was here, month after month, she would sit, rocking back and forth in her seat, cooing to the corpse of young Aesop, and speaking to him as if he were merely resting in his fresh new casket. In fact, this bizarre situation seemed to be the only recourse to be taken;

otherwise, theorized the husband, the woman might descend into a bottomless chasm of melancholy, and mourn herself to death.

Of course, the situation couldn't remain as it was. Bizarre happenings started to transpire in the home, as weird footsteps and strange knocks began to disturb the family and other visitors. Cold spots lingered, whispers could be heard barely audibly in the strange corners of the house when all was quiet. Mr. Wilson, though understanding the comforting effect of having the interred body of her son ever ready and at hand to speak with and comfort her, began to pressure Mrs. Wilson that, finally, something must be done. She would, at first, have none of it; after all, she had taken to spending her evenings hovering over the casket, talking to her baby, and doing her knitting. We could, perhaps, presume she was working on a burial blanket.

However, the bizarre manifestations continued, and even began to become increasingly worse, until it became quite apparent that some immediate action must be taken. Mr. Wilson finally decided to contact a Spiritualist from Louisville, Kentucky, to come up and officiate at what would become a séance—although history does not leave to us the identity of this august personage, we can well-imagine what the situation must have looked like. The average "sitting" consisted of several persons sitting around a table, in a dimly lit or darkened room, holding hands. Often, an old-fashioned séance could begin with a prayer, or with the singing of a hymn, but soon the officiating medium would begin to be "taken over" by a "control" or guardian spirit that would act as an intercessory between the sitters and whatever spirit they were attempting to contact (if, indeed there was any particular spook they were endeavoring to call up, and usually there was).

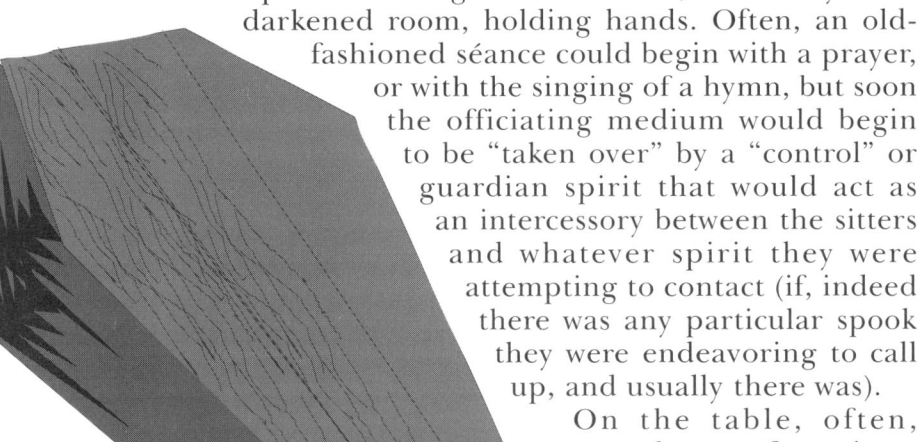

On the table, often, was a host of various odd assemblies: musical instruments (most often trumpets), and most especially items that could be considered to have been very important to the deceased spirit

being contacted; items like a pair of gloves, a lock of hair, a favorite trinket or broach.

Incidentally, some mediums well-versed in the "materialization" of entire spirit forms (ostensibly through the use of "ectoplasm," a sort of gooey mess that at times projected itself from the mouth, ears, or nostrils of the medium) had recourse to a "spirit cabinet," or a kind of wardrobe that could be entered by the spiritualist, and from which the "spirit form" would soon emerge. Of course, the incredulous (such as debunker Harry Houdini) could be forgiven for an amount of skepticism concerning the use of such trick cabinets, but the legitimate mediums did manage to produce a startling amount of truly inexplicable phenomenon: levitations, strange scents, weird tapping and rapping, musical instruments seemingly playing themselves, and so on and so forth. In addition, there were the spirit voices that seemed to mimic, perfectly, the voices of the departed. Often, these voices related information that could only be known to the grieving loved ones.

Such seems to have been the case in the Wilson séance. The anonymous medium settled himself down at the table, perhaps enjoining the family to first say a prayer, calling on the "highest of the high" to come forth and make itself manifest. After a suitable interval, the medium just having begun to feel the cool presence of spirit enter the room, the temperature must have dropped perceptibly. Suddenly, his "control" (a "red Indian") took possession of him, and to act as the "go-between" between the spirit being summoned, and the sitters.

In this case, we can surmise (and history records) that the spirit of Aesop Wilson made himself manifest. The mouth of the medium may have been moving, uttering the words in trance, or the message may have been given through "direct-voice" (i.e., the voice of Aesop Wilson might have come) like a soft, rustling whisper through the darkness, imploring: "Mother, bury me, for it is time for you to let go, and move on. And it is time for me to go to quiet rest."

Whatever, exactly, happened in that dark, séance room, we can be sure of one thing. Aesop Wilson's request to be buried, like other men, was finally heeded, and the family, henceforth, experienced no more disturbances.

4

Mary Roff
and Lurrancy Vennum

One of the strangest stories in the long, paranormal history of the Hoosier state involves the poignant tale of a young girl, seemingly possessed by forces outside the control of her ability to cope with—and the capacity of medical and psychiatric science to adequately explain.

Demonic possession, an idea as old as man and his recorded history, is a rare enough occurrence, but always a harrowing one. The few studies that have come down to us (mixed, of course, with the sensationalistic fare proffered by such things as *The Exorcist* and *The Omen*) offer an insight into a world both shocking and repellent: a world of foul, debased individuals who become the nexus of psychic maelstroms of profanity, violence, sickness, stench, and psychokinetic frenzy that can result in the insanity or death of the subject (not to mention the fatal effects it can have on the exorcist and his assistants, often many years later).

The Middle Ages is replete with "Devils of Loudon" and other familiar tales of otherwise orderly Holy Sisters suddenly tearing their garments, rolling on the ground, exposing their genitals, grunting like pigs, and hailing Satan. In modern times we might account for such manifestations as the outcome of group hysteria; the pent-up sexual frustrations of the physically and psychologically repressed. In modern times, we turn to psychiatry and the science of the mind to explain aberrant and seemingly demonic behavior. But not always

In the mid-seventies, a beautiful young woman from West Germany named Annelise Michele (whose names bears a poignant similarity to that of the famous Nazi victim Anneliese Michelle Frank), suddenly began to exhibit symptoms of hysteria, and complain of being attacked, late at night, in her room. It was not long before she became a bedridden wretch, began to speak in unfamiliar languages, proclaimed the spirits of Hitler and Judas Iscariot possessed her, and refused all food. During an aborted attempt at exorcism, the young girl starved,

literally to death. The priests were later tried for negligent homicide, but their sentences were comparatively light. Anneliese Michele died, incidentally, on the birthday of this author.

However, what if the offending spirit or spirits possessing the unlucky subject should be, not the spirits of infernal demons or evil dictators, but that of a fellow human who has just died, one that was unknown to the person being possessed? What would this suggest about the nature of human mortality? That souls "reincarnate?" That we are all simply manifestations of a vital, conscious energy, seeking a body, lifetime, after lifetime, to fulfill some purpose the likes of which even our discorporate spirits could not possibly imagine? And who decides who "goes on," to the light, and who remains? These are troubling questions.

More troubling in the case of Mary Roff, a young girl who plays no small part in the story we are about to unfold, although it is her death at the beginning of the tale that sets the stage for what comes later.

Born in Warren County, according to all accounts, Mary Roff lived to the age of nineteen before she began exhibiting bizarre, hysterical behavior. She began to convulse into epileptic fits, slash herself, speak angrily in a variety of bizarre voices, and became the center of occasional "rappings" and "knockings" about the house that could never be adequately explained. Her family, worried sick about her condition, consulted an alienist, who pronounced grimly, that it was entirely possible that the young woman would eventually have to be consigned to a sanitarium. The family, at a loss, stalled for time, and the bizarre manifestations and strange, maniacal shifts in mood continued.

Then, just as suddenly as they had come, they seemed to cease altogether, much to the relief of the Roff family, Things became so cheery and normal, for a short while anyway, that the family decided it was high time for a holiday. They went to visit friends in Peoria. And that was when the real trouble started.

Mary Roff degenerated rapidly, becoming a foul, cursing, hysterical monster, before finally succumbing to what may have been suicide. The family, heart-stricken, found themselves at a loss, but returned to Indiana with the body of their daughter to give her a burial more peaceful, at least, than the agony of her demise.

Fifteen months earlier a young girl by the name of Lurrancy Vennum had been born in Watseka, in 1864, to a perfectly normal family. It was thirteen years before young Lurrancy began to exhibit the same strange symptoms that young Mary Roff had exhibited before she died. The two, obviously, had never known of each other.

One of the most curious examples of the phenomenon that afflicted Lurrancy was bizarre physical contortions: Her body would bend, like a bow, until her the top of her head touched her heels. Also, upon being examined by a doctor, she began to speak in curious voices, flew out of a chair, and collapsed, as stiff as a board, into the arms of the doctor, seeming to weigh much more than her slim frame would suggest. For anyone who has ever read *Hostage to the Devil* by the late priest, Father Malachi Martin, or similar such books, the symptoms of demonic manifestation are unmistakable.

The girl began to complain of strange, brightly illuminated beings circling her bed, much in the manner that Mary Roff had once complained. The doctors all found themselves baffled, but the weird psychic phenomenon exhibited by Lurrancy Vennum so excited certain reporters that stories went out in the local papers. It was not long before the Roffs, by now certainly over their long period of grief for young Mary, were astounded to be reading of a case so very similar to that of their departed daughter. In no short time they contacted the Vennum family, and the two families finally met.

They suggested the intervention of a Dr. Stevens, a trained alienist from Wisconsin. He agreed to a consultation, and found the young girl sitting in a rocker, staring eerily off into space. In a scene that will remind modern readers of something out of *The Exorcist,* the young girl immediately snapped her neck around, growled at him in a foreign language, and said:

"Keep away from me! I'm Kristina Hogan, and I've just come here from Germany by sailing through the air!"

"Well," asked the cautious Doctor, "How long do you think you'll be staying with us?"

"I can stay as long as I like, but I'll be here for three weeks, if it's all the same to you!"

The conversation ambled on for a short while, Lurrancy mumbling in a number of strange voices, until, finally, she rose from her chair and began to exclaim: "Get out of here! Get out of here, all of you! There are too many of you, and I don't want you here anymore!"

The young girl fell over on the floor, again her body as stiff as a board and quite immovable. She continued to speak, and Dr. Stevens then asked her:

"Wouldn't you like to be controlled by someone a little nicer to you?"

Suddenly, out of the cacophony of strange sounds and weird names coming out of her mouth, Lurrancy's voice broke through.

"Yes, I would. There are some here with us that are not so bad."

Then after a short pause she stated.

"Mary Roff is here."

The father of the dead girl reportedly gasped, and then exclaimed, "Yes, have Mary come. We sure would like to speak with her again."

Lurrancy began to speak to "Mary."

"Mary, would you like to come and speak to your parents again?"

Suddenly, a new voice came trilling out of the mouth of Lurrancy Vennum. It was the voice of a young girl, and was instantly familiar to the Roffs. We can only imagine the great emotional turmoil this must have put both families in.

"I'm here now, Pa. I'll take the place of all the others."

Then Lurrancy smiled, sighed, and seemingly fell into a deep sleep.

This, however, was only the beginning of the story.

The family of Lurrancy Vennum was shocked that next morning when their daughter came to breakfast, expressed no memory of knowing any of them, insisted her name was "Mary Roff," and told them flatly that she *wanted to go home*.

Quickly, Mr. Thomas Vennum went down the street to the Roff home, knocked feverishly on the door, and informed the startled family of this new development. After a hasty consultation, it was decided to take no action for several days. After all, neither family had any way of knowing if this current possession was simply a passing fancy, or if indeed it was a special case worthy of drastic measures.

For several more days, Lurrancy continued to act, every bit, the role of Mary Roff, and insisted that she needed to go home and be with her real family.

Finally, after the girl seemed to lapse into a state of despondency, Thomas Vennum went back to the Roffs, informed them of the situation, and it was agreed that he should be accompanied back to the house by Mrs. Roff and her eldest daughter, Minerva.

Upon seeing Mrs. Roff and Minerva approach from up the street, Lurrancy (or rather, "Mary") leapt to her feet in a fit of joy, went to the door, flung it open, and raced across the yard to embrace Mrs. Roff with tears streaming down her face.

"Oh Mother! Oh, it's so good to see you again. Oh, how I've missed you! And *Nervie* has come too, I see."

The importance of this last remark was not lost on Mrs. Roff, who knew that Mary's pet name for her older sister had always been "Nervie." There was no way, of course, that Lurrancy could have known that (or anything else concerning the life of Mary Roff, for that matter).

When they were all settled inside, the following conversation stunned Mrs. Roff to the core of her being.

"Oh Mother," said Mary, "Do you remember the wonderful parcel of letters that I kept from my closest friends, right before I died? Did you keep those letters?"

Tears streaming down her face, Mrs. Roff said,

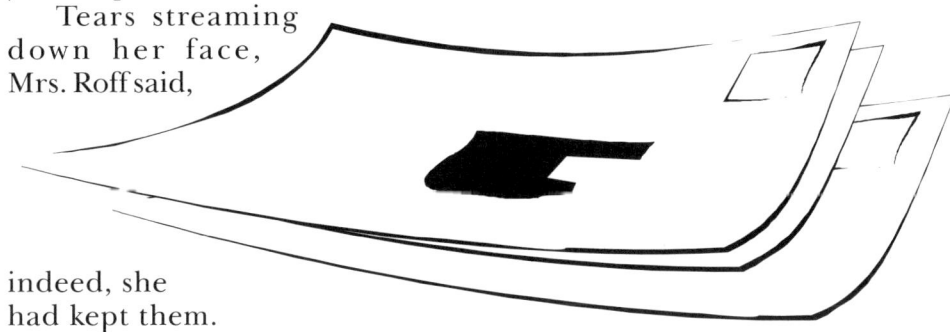

indeed, she had kept them.

"Mary" continued: "Mother I can tell you so many things about those letters, and I can prove to you that I am who I say. If you'll only go and check the letters, I'll give you all the information that you need…"

Indeed, a quick perusal of the letters in question confirmed all the particulars that Lurrancy (or rather "Mary") had told Mrs. Roff about their contents. The two families were now utterly convinced. But what to do about such a strange, enigmatic dilemma?

Of course, there was no question but that the girl would have to go and live at the Roffs, at least for the time being.

"Mary" told them, "The angels tell me I may stay until May. That's when Lurrancy will have to come back. I'm afraid I'll have to go again after that."

"But, where has Lurrancy gone, Mary?" asked an understandably concerned Mr. Vennum.

"She is being healed and restored spiritually. When she is ready, she will return, and I will have to go. Until then, I can stay. That's all that I'm allowed to tell you."

Indeed, for the next three months, Lurrancy Vennum lived, day and night, with the Roff family, as their departed daughter returned

"from beyond." She was, in every respect except physical, their daughter Mary Roff, and her every mannerism and utterance bore testimony to this fact. There was no deceit (whether conscious or unconscious) on the part of Lurrancy Vennum; she simply *was* their late daughter.

She correctly identified family members she could never have known, picked out photographs and incidents from her childhood, and described memories that only Mary Roff could have ever had any knowledge of. The carefully-preserved possessions of Mary Roff were handled by Lurrancy Vennum as if they had always been hers, and she had just been separated from them for a little while. She even knew when she had acquired them, and where.

She also, poignantly perhaps, described her own funeral. She related an incident that had happened in a room between Mr. and Mrs. Roff that *no one* else could have known.

One day, during the strange fifteen weeks that "Mary" was allowed to "live again," she was conversing with Dr. Stevens and the girl suddenly piped up strangely.

"Would you like to know how Emma is, Doctor Stevens?"

Dr. Stevens was taken aback. He indeed had had a daughter named Emma that had died several years earlier.

"She is ever so happy. She misses you though, and she says she would like to be with you and Mother again, if she could."

She went on to describe Dr. Stevens' late daughter completely accurately, even down to an obscure birthmark. Dr. Stevens later chronicled all this in his book, *The Watseka Wonder*.

The story of Lurrancy/"Mary" generated much interest at the time, and a good amount of press. The story was well-documented, and not a few local curiosity-seekers must have traveled by the Roffs to see if they could get a glimpse of the mysterious "Mary."

Finally, perhaps a little sadly, the spirit of Mary Roff, which had been occupying the body of Lurrancy Vennum for over three months, announced to the family that it would be time for her to be leaving soon.

"I must go, and let Lurrancy come back. She is nearly ready, and she is so homesick for her Ma and Pa."

"Mary" then leaned forward, shuddered, and seemed to fall into a deep trance. It was April 16th, 1878.

When the girl rose from her slump, both families (the Vennums had been brought over, for "Mary" had given them the exact date she would be leaving Lurrancy's body) were astounded to realize that "Mary Roff" was now gone; Lurrancy had returned.

Lurrancy expressed the feeling that she had felt as if she had just woken up from a "long sleep," and she seemed more than a little confused. She returned to the Vennum home, seemingly no worse for having been "away" for several months. Order was restored, we must assume, to both households, and baffled researchers were no closer to having understood what transpired during the entire long, strange episode than they are to this very day.

As for Lurrancy, she went on to marry, raise a family, and live to the ripe old age of seventy-six. She was still alive in 1940, though she was often reticent to speak of the strange experience of her past and the odd interval when her body, apparently, was possessed by the soul of a girl who had died long ago.

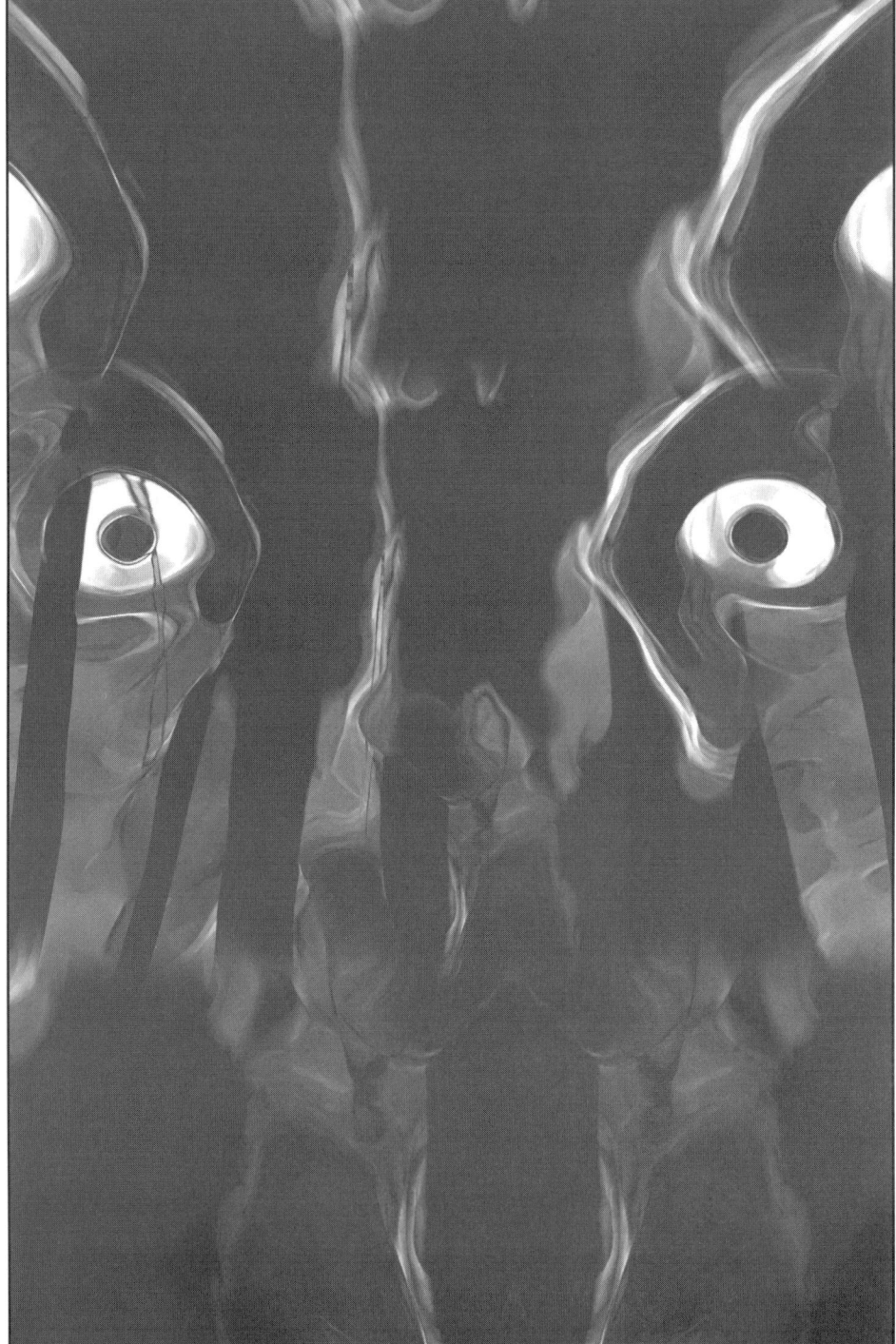

5

Attack of the Hairy Whatsits

It is an indisputable fact that, every so often, someone trekking through a graveyard, the woods, an abandoned swamp, or even an old dumping ground, will run across a creature or being that cannot be explained away in rational terms. Often, these threatening apparitions appear to be every bit as real as you or I, and, though they are invariably most often bipedal, they are NOT human in any recognizable sense of the word.

Often, these encounters with Hairy Whatsits will end one of two ways: with the creature being terrified into an instantaneous retreat or disappearance, or with the person experiencing the encounter fleeing for their life, either on foot or in an automobile, in sheer panic. The fleeting, terrifying nature of these encounters leaves them open, later, speculation about the experience. Is it simply some sort of hysterical spontaneous hallucination, or is it a glimpse of some secret race, some forlorn species that evolution bypassed or mutated out of all recognition to normal man? We may never know the answer to this question.

A trio of young kids gathered at the edge of an old cemetery in Blue Springs. Carefully, each one of them scaled the old fence, feeling the rough, dew-damped turf beneath their sneakers as they made their way through the old necropolis, laughing inwardly, and shivering a little at the daring boldness of their midnight prank. And did the moon shine brightly on their little shoulders as, hunched low, they moved through the overgrown grasses and atop the little mounds and hills that hid moss-covered monuments and leaning tombstones? Or, was it a pitch-dark night that held most of its secrets in its tightened grasp?

Again, we may never know.

It wasn't long, though, before the group was stopped, stone cold, in its tracks. For, rustling behind the overhanging branches of a willow, emerging like a nightmare from the marble magnificence of an august monument, came a form, covered in silver.

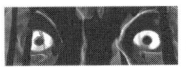

Its eyes glowed boldly in the night, and its massive frame seemed to be covered in hair from head to toe. The young children found themselves struck as if by a bolt of lightening (as is often the case in such manifestations) and had a scant few seconds to take in the unearthly weirdness of the massive being that reared itself before them. Then they took to their heels screaming, each trying to beat the other to be the first out of the cemetery, away to a place of safety, to a place warm and bright, where massive ape men with fiery eyes were still the stuff of comic books and horror films.

All of them swore, later, to the reality of what they'd seen.

Of course, we shouldn't be surprised. The Hoosier State has known the terrific stride and massive tread of "Bigfoot," or *Sasquatch* (or whatever designation the reader wishes to consign to this elusive half-man that is associated, chiefly, with the Pacific Northwest). He has been sighted in woodland areas on a number of various occasions down through the decades, and, though there is still no general consensus as to what he (or rather *it*) actually is or if it even exists in any tangible sense at all, one thing is for certain: To the various witnesses who have had the distinct pleasure of experiencing his company firsthand, even for a brief while, he is not a character that is soon forgotten.

We can reach backward through time, to the good year 1839, for Indiana's first recorded sighting of Bigfoot. Or can we?

The *Michigan City Gazette* made references to a small, grey, pseudo-ape: a thing that "whined piteously," was covered in fur, stood four feet tall, ran at an impressive gait, and when encountered, made piteous attempts to open verbal communication. Save for a few hardy, brave souls, one can well imagine these attempts were met by locals

bearing solid rounds of buckshot, but, at any rate, the thing, whether it was an unidentified animal or a feral human (four feet is awfully small to be considered a "Bigfoot" one would think), it was not again sighted for a good many years.

In 1883, a Mrs. Frank Coffman came upon a Hairy Whatsit while in the process of said creature picking bark, idly, from a tree, in a forest near Lafayette. Scared, the creature took off into the surrounding brush. It was not long before a large search party was assembled in pursuit of the mysterious beast, but it was to no avail.

The creature was described as long of arm, female of contour, and completely covered in fur.

A further sighting in 1897, likewise, elicited no captive specimen for the perusal of scientists, carnival goers, or just plain curious folk.

We next hear reports of our Hairy Man during the late forties and into the early fifties, in Boone County, and near Pulaski County, when various groups of people (including some children) recognized the furry presence of this seemingly-deathless woodland sentinel. Variously described as "between five foot and ten foot tall" at various times, the witnesses apparently did all agree on one thing: It looked like a bizarre crossbreed between man and primate.

Also, that it was terrifying.

Of course, the tracks of the creature are another strange calling-card left in the wake of this enigmatic animal, and they, combined with the oft-reported "screams in the dark" that many attribute to the howls of Bigfoot, have followed some residents of haunted Indiana down through the decades.

During the creepy decade of the sixties, not surprisingly, Bigfoot sightings took on a new, wilder dimension. Sixteen-inch footprints were recorded, wild shrieks filled the night in many rustic areas abutting forest, and the local populace of rural Indiana townships reported encounters with the creature. Many of these sightings involved reports of seeming "strange lights" in the sky, or UFOs. In one case, the bodies of two dogs were found to have been mutilated.

A word of caution to the would-be investigator: Whatever these Hairy Whatsits are, it would appear that, strictly speaking, they aren't exclusively vegetarian.

One of the strangest cases we're inclined to relate involves a Hairy Whatsit (or Bigfoot, if you like) and the strange phenomenon associated with UFOs, the occupants of which have, though very rarely, been said to resemble in many respects our big-footed bipedal beasts.

In Rising Sun, Indiana, in an area where UFOs and strange lights had occasionally been seen on the rural back roads, a Mr. Lester Kaiser lived in an old farmhouse with his wife and son, George. The year was 1969.

A mysterious power outage had troubled the family on May 18th, but had seemingly resolved itself by the next day. It was the very next day, though, while going out to do his chores, that young George, accompanied by his dog, happened upon a sight he would not soon forget.

As quoted in *The Complete Guide to Mysterious Beings*, by John A. Keel:

> *"It stood in a fairly upright position although it was bent over in about the middle of its back, with arms about the same length as a normal human being [...] I'd say it was about five feet seven or eight, in between there, and it had a fairly muscular structure. The head sat directly on the shoulders and the face was dark black, with hair which stuck out on the back of its head; had eyes set close together and a very short forehead. It was all covered with hair except for the back of the hands and the face. The hands looked like normal hands, not claws."*

George, panicking, apparently made a move to run and hide in the family automobile, but the creature posed no threat to him. It merely grunted and seemed to bound away, into the surrounding brush, and disappear.

The next day a Mr. Rolfing, a close neighbor of the Kaiser family, watched a brilliantly lighted blue and green object hover over a nearby field through binoculars. It was, in his opinion, a classic UFO. The problem of course, as John A. Keel poses in his book, is: Does one event have anything to do with the other?

Keel postulates that UFOs, Bigfoot, lake monsters, ghosts and nearly ALL other forms and manifestations of the unexplained are simply part of what Charles Fort would describe as the same "all-inclusive cheese." That is, that they are physical manifestations of an energy force in the electromagnetic realm that we cannot normally see, but that manifests itself in a variety of different ways to ordinary humans and has been doing so since the beginning of recorded history (and probably before that, too).

Thus, one phenomenon often follows the other (UFOs abut incidents of psychic precognition and "channeling," Bigfoot are often seen to swarm about UFOs, UFOs can often be sighted near reportedly "haunted" graveyards, and so forth), in an unbroken chain of weird occurrences and baffling happenings.

Of course, if some strange intelligence IS communicating through this sort of phenomenon, then what, pray tell, is the message hoping to convey? And why does it often pick the most terrifying guises it can muster (assuming it shape-shifts to meet our expectations) to try and convey said message?

Of course, a more logical explanation (but one that will not, in any case, satisfy the skeptics either), is that the Bigfoot, *Sasquatch*, *Yeti*, and all such "Hairy Whatsits" are simply a lost tribe of man, or some strange species of animal that we simply haven't discovered or uncovered yet. Such discoveries have confounded science before, such as when the *coelacanth*, a strange breed of fish long thought to have been extinct, was found to still be in existence. Could not our Hairy Whatsits simply be some evolutionary offshoot of mankind that has managed to tuck itself away in mountain (the *Yeti* has been described by Tibetan monks as well as Americans) and forest lo these many millennia?

If so, then next time you go hiking in the woods, take special care: There may be something lurking in the brush watching you. It may be confused, frightened, aggressive. It doesn't understand the strange roaring technology of our modern world: the paved roads, the rumbling trucks, or the hairless denizens of our age of scientific wizardry. It may not be able to wrap its rather evolutionarily limited brain around what species you are, and why your skin is smooth, and furless. But it does know one thing:

It's *always* hungry.

6

The Hartford Visitors

Color this one indelibly strange.

A young couple, the Donathans, were driving the lonely highways of Indiana near Hartford City back from a visit with the in-laws, when suddenly, while rounding the bend on a desolate stretch of road, they encountered what they first took to be "two children playing, wrapped up in aluminum foil."

Screeching to a halt in panic, the couple got a much better look at the two strange little beings they had encountered. They came to two startling realizations.

The first realization being that they were, most definitely, not children who had, somehow, been abandoned in the country to wander aimlessly and get themselves killed.

The second realization was that the two beings were, quite possibly, not even human.

The Donathans described, incredibly, two small creatures, both of whom could measure little more than four feet tall, and both dressed in immaculate silver suits. Though they were vague on description of the face, it was suggested that the heads were ovoid, and the eyes abnormally large. The arms were described as abnormally long and thin, reaching well below the waist.

What's even more bizarre is the way the creatures reportedly moved. It was a sort of slow-motion "hopping" movement, with the arms flapping up and down as if the two were, somehow, experiencing gravity in an entirely strange, new way. Additionally, Mrs. Donathan remembered the beings as having "boxlike" feet.

The strange little men hopped out of the headlights glow into the surrounding brush, and the Donathans quickly sped on, terrified. They stopped at a local café for a moment, trying to decide what on earth to do about the experience they had just had, before deciding to report it to the Hartford City Sheriff.

Deputy Sheriff Ed Townsend, along with a State Patrolman and another fellow, a local named Gary Flatter, were all present at the station, and became privy to the Donothan's strange report. Having no reason to suspect the couple of having confabulated the weird account, the three men took off to the particular section of road to investigate.

After driving for some time, the only phenomenon they could ascertain as being out of the ordinary was a bizarre, high-frequency "hum" or buzzing. Otherwise, they found nothing. Deputy Townsend decided to return to town, but the other two men decided to continue driving and searching for the two strange little individuals.

Since they had each, individually, taken their own vehicles, they split up, the state patrolman driving further east than the spot where the two beings had initially been seen, while Mr. Flatter (described as being a local who operated a filling station) continued to cruise the roads in the immediate vicinity, hoping for a glimpse of the mysterious critters.

He very soon got his wish.

Coming down a particular stretch of back road, he was forced to stop by what appeared to be a procession of fleeing animals, all "spooked" or terrified by the presence of something lurking in the woods. Mr. Flatter quickly drove to the side of the road, pulling over, and there, in the bright shine of his headlights, almost too glaringly brilliant to look at owing to the reflection of their strange costumes, were the two beings. Mr. Flatter added considerably to the description of the two visitors by noting the presence of a long hose coming down from the face, as if the two were wearing suits that amounted to diving suits or (perhaps more appropriately) "space suits." He also noted the boxlike boots the frail, tiny figures wore, and the peculiar egg-shaped heads they possessed.

Mr. Flatter decided, at first, to hit the two beings with his spotlight, but that idea quickly turned out to be the wrong one, as the tight-fitting, shiny suits they wore proved to make them too bright to be clearly visible. Mr. Flatter, was able to view them for awhile, apparently without a sense

of fear or trepidation, and he noted that the arms seemed to end with no hands, and that they "hopped," flapping their arms a bit while doing so. They reportedly could make terrific leaps.

After hopping for him several times, the strange beings hopped upward, disappearing into the darkness. Mr. Flatter then, reportedly, saw several brilliant flashes of red light in the night sky, but nothing else that was tangible. Whoever (or whatever) the two little beings had been, or where they had come from, remains a mystery to which, most probably, we may never know the answer.

7

The Dream
that Captured a Killer

This bizarre story comes to us from Indianapolis, a city with no small amount of weird tales emerging from its long, sordid history. This particular tale involves one of the most fascinating aspects of the human condition: the experiences of some individuals who have precognitive dreams, or similar visions.

Can someone dream something that is going to happening, or that happened somewhere far away from where they were busily snoozing? This is a peculiar and tricky question. Doctors J.B. and Louisa Rhine spent much of their professional lives investigating and documenting such anomalous occurrences as prophetic dreams, deathbed visions, ghosts, poltergeists, etc. Of course, the vast majority of precognitive dreams and psychic experiences are entirely mundane. In example, you dream of an old friend you haven't seen for some time, and then, within a day or two, out of the blue, they happen to call or drop by. Perhaps a remarkable coincidence?

This Indianapolis case most certainly does not involve a coincidence. While not strictly classifiable as "precognitive" (in that it doesn't seemingly involve a "future" event), it is certainly classifiable as an example of a psychic encounter with the unknown.

Mr. Joe Ammer was a hardworking, much-loved immigrant from Syria, who operated a shoe repair shop in a rundown section of Indianapolis. Joe was well-liked by his customers, was married to a good woman, and his son had just graduated from high school and was, most certainly, headed to college on a sports scholarship. Joe was sixty-seven years old in 1963.

One day, around noontime, while Mrs. Ammer was taking a nap, she had a strange dream. In it, she saw her husband, Joe, seeming to struggle with a man who was clearly wielding a hammer. In fact, he was being beaten by the man with the hammer, and after a moment, he crumpled to the floor of his shop.

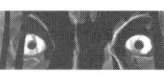

Mrs. Ammer woke up screaming.

Then, in a panic, she looked at the clock. The immediate relief she felt of waking up and being free of the nightmare was replaced by an eerie sense of foreboding. Her husband was late for lunch, which he always took at home.

She decided to wait, nervously, for a little while. Finally, she prepared a basket of food, and headed out to the shop. The basket was unnecessary; the food would never be eaten.

When she got to the shop, she went inside. She found the door to the back storeroom hanging open. She went into the dimly-lit room. She must have screamed. She certainly dropped the basket.

There, lying in a fresh pool of blood, lay the dead body of her husband. His hands had been bound behind his back with some string, and his skull had been savagely pummeled in. The killer's take from the entire robbery had been only a few dollars. Immediately, perhaps hysterically, the woman alerted the police.

At first, they found themselves to be skeptical concerning the idea that Mrs. Ammer had seen the killer in her dream only a short time before. But, she was able to give such a detailed description of the alleged murderer that they were forced to pay attention. Some astute officer took down her description, perhaps only as a kindness, and then got busy investigating the incident in the routine manner.

They weren't long in waiting for a break. An anonymous tip came in from an informant that a man, one William Edmonds, had entered a tavern only a few minutes after the beating death of Joe Ammer. He had apparently hustled his way to the restroom, and busily tried washing the blood from his hands. This witness described Mr. Edmonds in nearly exactly the same way as had the dreaming Mrs. Ammer, and the police detectives were all, truly, astounded.

Edmonds was arrested, and after a speedy trial, was sentenced to life imprisonment. He had reportedly committed the robbery and murder for drug money.

A true-life case from the borderland of the unexplained.

8

Lady Wonder
Knew the Answer

How intelligent are animals? Are they gifted with psychic abilities in much the same way that human beings are? If so, are some animals intelligent enough to communicate what they know to their human masters? This next case raises these unsettling (and some would even say absurd) questions to a new level.

Ronnie Weitcamp was playing with three young friends in the backyard that October 11th of 1955, when, for some unknown reason, he decided to stray alone into the woods. After several minutes, his young friends, perturbed at his continued absence, went into the Weitcamp home to complain to Ronnie's mother that, "He went into the woods and won't come out."

Ronnie's mother was instantly frantic with concern, for the Weitcamps lived near the Crane Naval Depot, a hilly south-central Indiana area known for hundreds of acres of timber and scrubland. After a few moments, panic set in upon the woman, and she called her husband and alerted the police.

Thus began the largest manhunt (until that time) in Indiana history: over 1,500 men, both law enforcement officers and workers at the naval Depot, combed every conceivable nook and cranny of the surrounding area for a three-mile radius, in a vain attempt at finding the boy. It was to no avail, and by nightfall the concern grew even greater, since it seemed unlikely that a boy like Ronnie Weitcamp would be able to survive such a cold night, alone in the woods.

Yet still they continued the search. The shocking news of the boy's disappearance left the community stunned, and a host of "Ronnie sightings" and wild rumors surfaced. That none of these tips and leads bore any substantiate evidence of the boy's whereabouts goes without saying; one dullard even suggested that the boy was buried in the backyard of his parent's home, a notion that was, in this case, of course false.

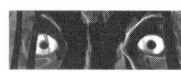

WTTV, the television station in Bloomington that was continually running Ronnie's picture in hopes that someone would recognize him and provide some valuable clue as to his disappearance, had at its news helm at the time one Frank Edwards, one of Indiana's most talented and mysterious sons. Mr. Edwards would go on to write a series of books, taking up where Charles Fort and Robert Ripley before him left off, by chronicling the astounding, strange happenings and supernatural events that occur in the lives of everyday folks. Then, having exhausted that, he began to chronicle the world of UFOs. (Frank Edwards was—and still is—a big inspiration to the present author.)

It was the intervention of Frank Edwards that, eventually, solved the mystery. Edwards had in his ever-burgeoning news files the story of a particularly fascinating animal, a horse that had, apparently, helped solve the mystery of another missing boy in Richmond, Virginia. The horse, known by her owner as "Lady Wonder," was trained to flip over a series of tin plates on a wire, each bearing a letter of the alphabet. It was in this way, the horse allegedly was able to answer questions put to her. But, even better than that, the horse apparently had a mysterious "sixth sense" that allowed her to know things that regular humans could not. It was in this manner that she had facilitated in finding the remains of a missing boy in Virginia, and it was this bizarre, true-life case that Frank now remembered as he busily dug through his file cabinet.

Upon finding the information he was looking for, he quickly made up his mind as to what to do. It took a few phone calls, but Frank finally secured both the cooperation of some trusted (though reluctant) friends and the assistance of the owner of Lady Wonder, who was only too eager to help out in any capacity that he could in such a special case.

As Edwards later related the scene, it was a very strange situation. The horse, when asked if she knew what her human visitors were there to find out about, trotted forward and, using her snout, flipped over a few of the tin letters, spelling out the word "boy."

The perplexed party then asked Lady Wonder the name of the boy in question. She again flipped the tin letters over to spell "Rone."

Spelling aside, this clearly meant the boy's name was "Ronnie."

They then asked if the boy still lived. The answer to this was, unfortunately, "No."

The horse continued to answer questions, describing a sandy ravine, under an elm tree, where the body would be found sometime in December. When asked if Ronnie had been kidnapped, the answer came back as "no." Apparently, according to Lady Wonder's prognostications at least, Ronnie had met death through sheer misadventure.

The interviewers left bewildered, and Frank Edwards now had a weird dilemma to deal with. What to do with the information? Should he keep it to himself, go to the police (who in no case could be expected to believe the predictions of a talking horse), or should he broadcast it on television, and risk the contempt and ridicule of thousands of outraged Hoosiers? He was a brave man, was Frank Edwards.

He chose to air the information from Lady Wonder on his news program, and was greeted with a storm of ridicule and stern condemnation from Indiana newspapers. In fact, if things had gone a little differently Frank might have ended up losing his job over the whole affair. After all, how must the grief-stricken parents of the missing boy have felt when a newscaster broadcast the prediction that their son's body would be found, based entirely on the supposed psychic faculties of a talking horse?

It was not long afterward though, that two hiking teenagers came across the remains of a small boy, in a sandy ditch, near an old elm tree. Apparently, the boy had fallen and injured himself. Unable to get back up again, he had died a terrible death of exposure. It was Ronnie Weitcamp.

The police quickly ascertained that he had not been kidnapped, and the state of his remains and their location matched, perfectly, with the predictions of Lady Wonder. Frank Edwards was vindicated, and skeptics were, momentarily, hushed.

Of course, this tale is a tragic one with a deeply sorrowful ending. The death of a child is always a tragedy. Tragedy, however, can often bear in its grasp the seeds of mystery and hope.

And Wonder.

9

Fearful Folktale

To begin with, no one can accurately vouch for the veracity of this particular yarn. However, whether it be true or not, it is a ghoulishly delightful little piece of folklore that has been handed down in Indiana for time out of mind, and thus bears repeating here.

Two old farmers sat together in a local bar in Versailles, getting pleasantly inebriated, and ribbing each other about their respective courage. One dared the other to spend the night in the local haunted house.

"You don't have the nerve to spend the night in that old place."

"You want to bet? I tell you, I'm as brave a man as any that ever lived, and I will prove it to you."

"Oh really?"

"Yes. Just drive me out to the old place, and you sleep out in the truck. I'll go inside and spend the entire night, It's a warm night, so you shouldn't have any problems. If I need any help, I suppose I can always holler out the door for you."

"And if you chicken out?"

"If I chicken out, you can have my prize heifer. If I do manage to spend the whole night, I'll take your prize calf. That should sweeten the deal. Are you game?"

"Sounds like a good idea to me. Let's do it."

So off they went. The old farmer crept up to the foreboding structure, cautiously, while his friend watched him from the cab of his beat-up old pickup truck. He settled in for a long night.

Just as he was about to drift off to sleep, he heard a horrifying scream shrieking through the night. His heart suddenly leapt into his throat, and grabbing his flashlight, he hurried to the door of the forbidding old place, threw the front door (which was leaning precariously on its rusted hinges) wide open, and strode inside, calling out his friend's name and casting the wide beam of his flashlight about until, suddenly, it fell upon the face of his friend.

It took his mind a moment to adjust to what he was seeing.

He stepped forward.

There was his friend standing by the fireplace. Only, he wasn't moving; his face seemed to be frozen still. In another, horrified moment, the old farmer realized why.

His head had been severed from his body and plopped, like a dripping morsel, upon the mantle. Blood and grue trickled from the mouth, running down the mantle and pooling at the bottom of the fireplace in a growing stream.

The old farmer screamed, dropped his flashlight, and ran for his truck, fumbling with the keys, and pulling away in a screech of burning rubber and a cloud of dust. He went directly to the Sheriff.

At first, the Sheriff greeted the story with some suspicion, suspected the man was drunk, considered throwing him in the tank with the other local winos, but then thought better of it. The man did seem to be, genuinely, scared out of his wits. Grabbing a deputy, the three men went back out to the old house, and the two law officers went before the cowering farmer, who was hard pressed to actually work up the nerve to go back inside the place.

To his amazement, when the three men entered, they immediately found the headless farmer standing in front of them, as healthy as the day he was born, and looking curiously puzzled.

He explained: "I actually lost my nerve right when I first came in, and snuck out the back entrance. Then I heard you yell and pull out in a hurry, and I wondered what was up. Now, you're back here with the Sheriff. You mind explaining this all to me?"

When the farmer who had witnessed the severed head began to stutter forth his astonishing encounter again, the men assembled grinned, putting it all down to a case of a yokel and his overactive imagination. Those who were more knowledgeable concerning the awful history of the house weren't so quickly dismissive.

The place had been the scene, apparently, of a horrible murder. A stout, seemingly-religious farming family had lived in the house for many years, and gave every appearance to

outsiders of being the sorts of folks that anyone would want to have as neighbors. It seemed, however, that trouble was brewing in the midst of them, apparently something of an unknown origin. One awful night, the father of the family went terribly insane.

He butchered his wife and children with an axe, and blew his brains out in the barn with an old shotgun.

Before his suicide, however, he had taken to beheading each of his children (and, we may presume his wife, as well), and placing their severed heads on the fence posts outside and in various parts of the house for the authorities to find later. It must have been an awful sight for whoever first found the massacre—to approach the home and have the severed heads of the children staring back at them from the fence as they walked up to the yard.

Of course, such a tragedy breeds tales of ghosts and haunting, and so it was that the old house was said to still hold the evil energy that had first driven the father of the family to his act of barbaric madness. Some say his ghost still walks the premises, axe in hand, blood dripping from the blade down his dirty fingers and leaving a spotty trail behind him as he goes. Others say that severed heads appear, sometimes floating, all around the place for anyone that dare visit.

That is, if such a house still exists in Versailles, Indiana. Or ever did.

10

Werewolves?

The very title of this chapter will make some people grin. After all, the very word "werewolf" conjures up images of Lon Chaney Jr. tied to a chair before a slow dissolve renders him a hulking, hair-covered product of Universal Studios makeup artist Jack Pierce. Or, alternately, one might be put in mind of such grade-b horror films as *Wolfen*, or *The Howling*. One does not, typically, think of the subject as having any basis in reality.

Well, it does. *Lycanthropy* is a classified mental illness whereby the afflicted actually believes themselves to be assuming the characteristics of a wolf. Anyone who has ever studied the history of serial killers, or their strange cyclical patterns will also pick up on the "wolf-like" or predatory nature of some bestial, psychopathic individuals. It is not, shall we say, a pleasant subject.

Through history, there have been cases of werewolves recorded by historians. One of the most famous cases of Lycanthropy (which also, coincidentally involved black magic and a pact with the Devil) was that of Peter Stubbe of Bedburg, Germany, sometime in the early Middle Ages. Stubbe, along with his mistress, a young woman named "Beel" (appropriately sinister, don't you think?) supposedly used the black arts to conjure up the living Devil, who granted them the use of a special leather belt which would enable Stubbe to transform himself into a werewolf.

Whether or not the reality of his alleged transformation can ever be ascertained, one thing is quite certain: His crimes (including incest) were certainly real enough.

Stubbe pounced upon unwary travelers, killing them, wolf-like, with his teeth and bare hands, and robbing them of their loot. He did this countless times, but one supposes the culminating episode in his sordid career was the butchery and cannibalism of *one of his own children*.

In short, he was never going to win any prizes for being "Parent of the Year."

Stubbe was captured, while in the act, and one assumes, took off and cast away his leather belt just in time to be captured in human

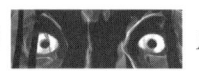

form. Unluckily for him, the authorities at the time were not an understanding lot, and mad as a hatter or not, he was quickly tortured. Convicted of being in league with the Devil and practicing the "Black Arts," he was broken on the wheel, tortured again with hot pincers, beheaded, and then his head was hung on a pole beneath a picture of a wolf—a warning for potential wrongdoers and those considering a similar pact with the forces of darkness. As for his mistress and daughters, they were likewise beheaded and burned at the stake.

Ah, justice flowed swiftly in those happy days.

More recent examples include a case from England investigated by none other than the famous parapsychologists Ed and Lorraine Warren, who provided an exorcism for a man who was allegedly possessed by the spirit of a wolf. The man would begin to lose his sanity, his ears would become pointed, his teeth would elongate, and hair would begin to sprout from his face. He would then act like an uncontrollable madman. Happily, in that case, the Warrens were apparently able to dispel the man's demon before he could get himself into serious trouble.

As for Indiana, there are two—yes, two—troubling werewolf or wolf-man accounts that we have to deal with. The first comes from Tippecanoe, and harkens back to the day when French Trappers first spoke the tales of men who, cursed by the Devil, were fated to become wolves when the moon was full.

According to the account of "A.K.B.," published in the Marshall County *Bourbon Mirror in* January of 1872, two strange, unexplained creatures, wolf-like, were seen to rampage the countryside in or around Devil's Swamp, south of Tiptown, tearing apart the animals of local farmers and shattering the night with piercing, maniacal screams. The beings were said to be hairy, wolf-like, and in possession of piercing, fierce eyes that burned red in the light of the full moon.

They were, in every respect, an unpopular menace, and the stuff of which legends were made and nightmares born.

Finally, on December 21, 1871, two men—Del Latham and J.H. Debolt—swallowing whatever fear they may have felt, set out with rifles, knives, and a pack of dogs to do the creatures in, and finally get to the bottom of the mystery concerning just what it was they really were.

After a hard, grueling pursuit of nearly two miles, both men found the odd creatures reposing in a wooded thicket, and immediately began shooting. They then closed in on the prey, brandishing knives, but the two creatures proved exceedingly difficult to kill.

Latham was beat about the skull by ferocious paws, immediately losing consciousness. Upon awakening, he found Debolt barely alive, with an arm nearly severed clean to the bone, and the gruesome signs of an titanic struggle littered about. The residue of exploded rifles, murdered and bloody dogs, torn branches, and the carcasses of at least one of the unknown creatures, were there, ready to be cleaned, claimed, or pondered.

Debolt survived his horrific wound, but was unlucky enough to lose his arm forever. As for the body of the creature, it was put on display (as was customary in those days) as a local curious attraction. The carcass of the beast was measured at six feet and nine inches in length, and nearly two and a half feet on all fours. It weighed a solid two hundred pounds.

The carcass was put on display at an unidentified general store, but the vicious fangs and claws were kept by a Dr. Hall for any number of years beyond counting. Unfortunately, for those who would check the veracity of this particular tale, the remains, and any knowledge as to what might have become of them, have long since vanished. Although, the town of Tiptown was still, reputedly, hanging on by a thread.

The other tale involves an erstwhile Confederate soldier known to history as "Silas Shimmerhorn." Silas was a native-born Hoosier who, while becoming lost from his regiment (who had come to Indiana to raid Union supplies) was unlucky enough to find himself smack dab in the middle of the local militia. Quickly hiding himself out in the woods, he took to sleeping in an old cave (referred to, locally, as the "Bat Cave"), and decided that his small part in the war between the states had come to an end. After a time, he took to liking the isolation so much, he made his condition a permanent one.

No one, at the time, could have blamed him. As a Confederate soldier in Indiana, his capture by enemy forces would have, almost certainly, resulted in him doing a short dance at the end of a long rope. At any rate, he lived in the cave, on what he could kill with his rifle and ever-dwindling supply of shot.

It was when this supply of shot ran out that the real trouble began. Fortunately, Silas Shimmerhorn still had his knife, and became reasonably skilled at hunting down small animals for food. Also, strangely, he managed to win the "friendship" of a small wolf pack that roamed the area, sometimes sharing his grub with them. They, oddly, began to accept him as one of their own, instead of seeing him (as one would expect) as an easy entrée. The fact that he finally doffed his regular, frayed and dirty clothing for a costume made entirely of furry hide might have helped.

It was at this time, or so the story goes, that Silas Shimmerhorn underwent an internal transformation as well as an external one.

He forgot the normal habits and mannerisms of man, perhaps even forgot the use of language, and let a powerful inner-beast come forth from the depths of his spirit and claim him. He became, in essence, a literal "wolfman," what the old-time French Trappers in Indiana would call a *loup-garous,* a shape-shifting man that could transform himself into the image of a wolf. The Native Americans believed in them, too (many who still practice the old traditions, we must assume, still give them credence), and sure enough, Native legends from Indiana abound with stories of the "shape-shifter."

(To be quite thorough however, it must be admitted that many of these *loup-garous* were not, strictly speaking, men-into-wolves, but could also be eagles, cows, chickens, toads, or anything else one can imagine.)

Thus, it would seem, the capacity for man to travel backward, along the route of evolution, could be exemplified by these special, supernatural cases.

Of course, the legend of children being "raised by wolves" is an endemic part of our history. Adam Parfrey, in his seminal underground anthology *Apocalypse Culture*, gives us the example of "Kamala" and "Amala"[1], two children found in the wild by an Indian doctor named Singh, who apparently rescued the two girls from a wolf den outside of Midnapore. His diary (which was later published), reveals a startling duo whose mental and *even physical* features had evolved to a wolf-like state. The two children walked on all fours (they, in fact, never could stand), their teeth had grown sharp and uneven, their eyes glowed, sharply in the dark, and they could smell meat from yards away.

Most interesting perhaps is the way in which he describes their jawbones, which "parted visibly" while chewing, unlike those of humans. Also, he swears, the insides of their mouths were blood red.

The two nearly-mutated "wolf children" soon died in captivity, unfortunately—but not unlike nearly every other similar case. It is as if, once the animal had been fully unleashed in them, they could no longer reclaim their "human" state, and the animal was all that was left. They died, each of them, of a "broken heart" or spirit, as it were.

In the case of Silas Shimmerhorn, though, his own personal saga has a much more mysterious ending.

Local farmers began to realize, soon enough, that there were wolves about: Mutilations of their livestock were becoming a troubling, regular occurrence. Yet, they also realized that something strange was occurring simultaneously: They would find a mixture of confusing tracks, those of a wolf, and those of an apparently barefoot *man*. There were also other indications that a human being was, astoundingly,

running and hunting with a pack of wolves—namely, the presence of a bloody knife found at the scene of one of the animal butcheries.

Soon, a posse was convened to track down the wolves, and also we must presume, to hunt down, capture, or even kill the lunatic that had, miraculously, managed to become part of the "pack."[2]

They were it would seem, entirely luckless upon this point. Although nothing specific was ever recorded, it came down through the years that many men sighted Silas Shimmerhorn, and that he had regressed into a wild, fur-wearing beast of a man, with long matted hair, claw-like nails, and sharp teeth. Tales have him running, wolf-like, braying at the moon, and generally behaving as much like a wolf as could be imagined. It was thought by some that Silas had managed to transform himself, from man to man-beast: a creature somewhere between braying wolf and deathless revenant.

Years later, another rash of mutilations brought back the disquieting tales of Silas Shimmerhorn, and there were those who swore they caught a glimpse of the barbaric hermit running through the woods like an animal, although by this time he must have been either incredibly ancient, or dead.

Perhaps he was immortal now, after all.

Even today, there are witnesses who claim you can hear still his piercing wail resound through Versailles State Park, and, if you are lucky (or perhaps unlucky), you can catch a glimpse of Silas Shimmerhorn—filthy, fur-clad, and looking every bit the veritable half-man, half-wolf—running through the forest, still searching and forever hungry.

11

The Vincennes Airship

F ew people weaned on television realize that the UFO phenomenon is nothing new, but is indescribably ancient, going back thousands of years into the dawn of pre-history. In fact, cave paintings at *Chichin-Itza* seem to suggest that primitive men were quite aware of the unearthly presence of *something* in the skies above them.

An even fewer number are aware that the once-popular (and often denigrating) term "flying saucer" was NOT coined by pilot Kenneth Arnold, who reported a formation of strange, disc-like aerial objects over Mt. Rainier, Washington, while he was flying a rescue mission in 1947.

In fact, the term "saucer" was coined by a farmer in Texas in 1878, who spotted a dark "saucer-like" object fly over his field one day, and was befuddled as to what its origin could possibly have been.

Most people (even those somewhat interested in "mysteries" or folklore of the paranormal) are not well-acquainted with the original UFO "wave" of sightings that occurred in America (across the Midwest) as early as 1897. These devices, while not being described as "disc-like," were, nonetheless, the first UFO reports largely documented in the United States.

The Airships (while undoubtedly some reports were hoaxes) would terrify a great many people, and according to author John Keel, would go on to inspire famous, early science fiction authors like H.G. Wells and Jules Verne to pen their respective classics *War of the Worlds* and *Master of the World*.

Whether that is the case or not, imagine, if you will, being a poor farmer in 1897. There are no airplanes, jets, and not that many balloons to speak of either. Suddenly you look up from your work to the clear, blue sky that seems to roll on across the fields forever.

Hanging there, as if by magic, is a monstrous, dark cigar-shaped object, roughly the equivalent of the Goodyear Blimp.

You might, even if you are not a curious man, stand up and take notice.

Such an event transpired in Vincennes in 1897. According to various sources, on Friday, April 16th, a strange, glowing "golden ball"

was first sighted by one individual over Union Depot around nine o'clock in the evening.

What followed was a litany of reports from various witnesses, all of whom described an object cigar-shaped, having a number of side-propellers, and moving like a "steamship" in the clouds. These witnesses, to a man, comprised some of the most respectable people in Vincennes at the time. The names include: Sam Judah, who watched the object move with "fluttering wings"(!) from his storefront property, a "Col. Ewing" who claimed to have seen a "bright golden ball" he took at first to be a falling star until it moved closer to his front porch, and a Victor Schonfeld who was a balloon enthusiast who had made several trips in the air himself (his word, therefore, being taken as reliable in regards to mysterious airships).

Whatever the object was, several unimpeachable witnesses (including a local judge) swore that, as it grew closer, they could well see, amidst all the bright, intense lights, the contours of what they took to be a cabin clinging to its underbelly. Some said they could hear talking, perhaps in a curious, unknown tongue[3], emerging from the cabin. Other's claimed they could see movement inside.

Whatever the case, according to the reports in the *Vincennes Morning Commercial*, the strange object made its way across town in a southeasterly direction before, gradually turning back around, and heading directly over what is, presently, known as Gregg Park. It is assumed that the Airship pilot (assuming that there was one) was taking his vehicle back the way it had come after a test run, or, alternately (perhaps frighteningly) was stopping for a landing.

This was not unknown in airship reports.

The reported landings by the Airship crewmen fit, unerringly, into a bizarre pattern. Usually, as in one case in Texas, they crew was happened upon while in the act of performing some "maintenance" or repair. The reports most often included normal-looking occupants, although the dress or clothing was often said to look strange to the eyes of people in 1897. Sometimes they were said to be "foreign" or even Oriental-looking. Often they were said to wear "smoked" glasses (old-fashioned sunglasses).

These bizarre crewmen also frequently had one other feature that seemed to distinguish them from ordinary folks: They often had abnormally (even grotesquely) long beards or whiskers. This fact is chronicled by John Keel in his excellent book *UFOs: Operation Trojan Horse*. Make of it whatever thou wilt.

Often, the landed airship crew would brag about how they could "be in Greece, tomorrow," since their machine was capable of such enormous speed. Also, they often hinted darkly of revealing themselves and their invention to the world, or engaging in current armed conflicts in other countries. Strange, truly.

In the case of the Vincennes Airship though, one good circle across town, putting themselves on display for the befuddled citizens, seems to have been sufficient publicity for the crew of this flying Rube Goldberg device. The mystery dirigible faded away into the nighttime sky, and secured itself a firm place in the pages of the unexplained.

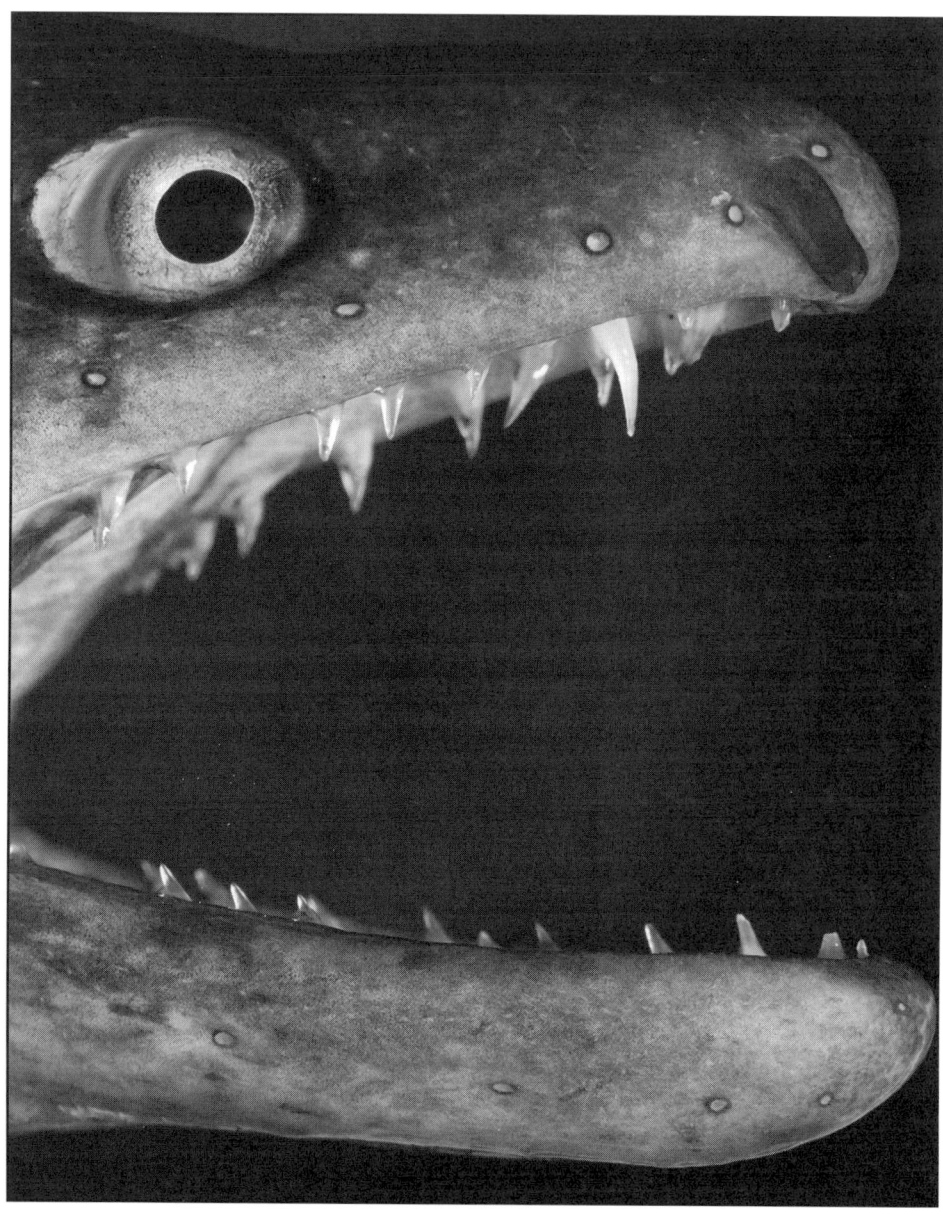

12

The Crawfordsville Monster

While we're on the subject of mysterious sights in the sky, it might do us well to visit the Crawfordsville Monster.

Two men were hitching a wagon one morning out in front of one of their houses, while the wife and kids were out sitting on the porch. Visiting at the time was the right Reverend G.W. Switzer, an individual who would come to play an important part in what happened later.

It was not long before one of the men noticed a strange object moving toward them from out of the sky, flying in a circular pattern. It seemed to be swooping down toward the house, but would then circle back up again. They, at first, thought it might be some sort of grotesque bird, but were soon disabused of that notion the closer it got. The horses began to rear up, and very soon the witnesses realized they were looking at something terrifyingly out of the ordinary: the Crawfordsville Wonder, or Monster, more properly.

The description of the monster itself varies, but it is beyond the capacity for most minds to conceive.

It was described as a twenty-foot-long, eel-like creature without a head, but with two glowing, red eyes at the end of its body. The creature was likewise said to have several fish-like fins running up and down the sides of its body, and to "undulate and squirm" as it went through the air.

Perhaps the creature was the sort of flying "gas-bag" postulated by Carl Sagan in his ground-breaking book, *Cosmos*, as a possible biological form for extraterrestrial life (if we should ever discover any). Whatever the case, the creature was said to give off a terrible "whine" or frightening wail, and then to disappear into the clouds, not to be seen again for several months.

Some accounts also describe the creature as belching smoke or smog.

Of course, this terrifying sighting unsettled the assembled to a great degree, but there seems to be little record on whether or not they told anyone outside of their assembled party about the sighting. Of course, this waould be entirely logical for (excepting perhaps, the Rev. Switzer) all of them would, immediately, have been taken to be liars or

worse. No, apparently they kept this strange encounter to themselves, leaving the community of Crawfordsville entirely unprepared for what was to happen next.

It was on September 9th, 1861, during broad daylight as the town went about the hustle and bustle of its daily business that someone first sighted a strange, squirming "thing" coming toward them from the clouds. Perhaps at first the rapidly growing group of witnesses in the street thought that a strange kite or pieces of balloon were drifting toward them out of the sky. They were soon disabused of this notion.

Imagine, if you will, the great, aerial serpent, nearly eight feet in width and twenty feet long, circling, like something from a Medieval fairy tale, over the small, stunned community, belching smoke and wailing its hideous banshee wail. Imagine the looks of horror on the faces of the people below as they caught sight of the massive, serpentine body, the fish-like fins, and the twin, glowing red eyes that seemed to be set in the center of the body[4] (for the thing had no head).

Over 100 people witnessed this last great exhibition of the aerial eel, the Crawfordville Monster, and they, to a person, gave the same description and account of the same creature, right down to the same strange, moaning wail. Some thought (or somehow got the impression) that the thing might have been sick, or injured. Whatever the case, it soon disappeared, leaving 100 stunned local witnesses to try and sort out for themselves whether or not what they had seen was actually real, or (as some have suggested), was simply a case of "mass hallucination" or mass hysteria.

As for the Crawfordsville Monster, this would be its final performance. Whether or not it died, slipped back to whatever dimension it slipped out of, or simply faded back into the fabric of human hallucinations, is unknown.

Interestingly, Charles Fort, the great early chronicler of such outlandish sightings, took the entire account to be a hoax, but nonetheless went about trying to locate the Rev. Switzer. To his shock and amazement, he found that, indeed, a Rev. Switzer had lived in Crawfordsville at the time, and, after some difficulty, finally located the extremely elderly man and struck up a correspondence with him.

The Reverend verified each of the sightings, personally, to Charles Fort.

Whatever the factual reality concerning the Crawfordville Monster's actual existence, the sightings of it, both of them, indeed *did* occur.

13

Headless Rider

We've all heard of the Headless Horseman, that strange phantasm that chased poor Ichabod Crane through a dark, Disneyland forest in a bygone cartoon that was inspired by the famous tale composed by American author Washington Irving.

What are we to make, however, of the Headless Horse*woman*? Perhaps Equal Opportunity has finally caught up with the world of spirits and ghosts. This tale comes to us from the very excellent book *Ghost Stories of Indiana* by Edrick Thay.

Back in the bygone, settler days of Indiana history, there was a young girl named Lucy. She was a pretty young lady, with long red hair and a turbulent temper to match. She lived on a farm in Wheatfield, and she was her parent's pride and joy. She was also their seemingly eternal source of grief and worry, as well.

Lucy possessed a temper so fiery, and a free spirit so naturally unbridled and untamable, that it more often than not erupted into stormy confrontations between herself and her father, who would roar at her as she stormed from the farmhouse out to the stable, and rode away for the night on her favorite horse.

These night rides were her source of comfort and her chief form of therapy. She would return from them calm, contrite, and ready to be an obedient daughter (as was expected from young ladies in that bygone age) once more.

Her parents, noticing the marked change in her after her evening (or sometimes late-night) rides, let her go. Of course, in hindsight they must have regretted that they didn't try to stop her, for what happened next can only be described as tragic.

It was early one night when the headstrong Lucy, suddenly, sprang upon her parents that she would be attending a local dance that evening. Her father immediately roared his disapproval. It was Saturday, and that was supposed to be "family day."

"You're not going and that is final!"

"I am, and there is nothing you can do to stop me! I'm not a baby anymore!"

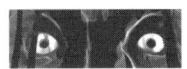

"I'm warning you, young lady, if you step foot out that door, you'll never enter this house again. Do you hear me? You'll never come back to us again, by God!"

Upon her father swearing this questionably profane oath, Lucy's mother burst into tears, and Lucy burst out the door. They knew full-well she was going for one of her "rides," and that she might not be back until dawn. They went to bed not suspecting the tragedy that would befall later, under the waning moon.

Lucy went to the stable, mounted her horse, and rode out under the dark clouds of night, going deep along the old dirt roads in the dim moonlight. She, at first, must have still been fuming. What happened then can only be conjectured.

Lucy may have begun to feel poorly about her harsh language and the poor treatment of he parents. Or she might have begun to feel a twinge of rare fear steal over her. Whatever the case, she unexpectedly decided to turn back. It would be her final decision.

Some say there may have been a maniac lurking in the woods, perhaps an escaped prisoner or a lunatic from a local asylum. Others said that the imprecation to God, delivered by her father only a short time earlier, had somehow decided her fate.

Whatever the case, whether it was a maniac or a short limb overhanging the road that, Absalom-like, caught the flowing, wild red hair in its branches, one thing is for certain: Poor Lucy managed to lose her head (literally) on her ride back home.

Her horse trotted back to the farm at daybreak, as her father was just getting up to his chores. He cursed himself for sleeping so late, and then realized, to his horror, that Lucy's horse had come home, but Lucy had not.

Quickly, he went into the woods to search her out. Later, he acquired a posse of neighbors to help in the search. One of them found a rather gruesome tableaux.

Hanging like a macabre lantern from the branches of a tree, was a severed head with long, red hair. The hair was tangled (or tied?) into the branches, and, below it, in a puddle of dried blood, was the body of poor, dead, rebellious Lucy.

The father was utterly shattered, his final words ringing in his ears like the death knell of his only daughter. The body was buried on the farm, but, of course, that was not the end of the tale, or we wouldn't be relating it here to you, in this book of weird legend and occurrences.

It is said by some who go through (what has now become) "Ghostly Hollow" in Knox County that, at times, when the moon is waning, you can hear the tremendous hoof beats of a galloping steed. If you wait a few moments there (perhaps shivering in your shoes), you will catch sight of something so bizarre and horrifying that you will never forget it for the rest of your natural life (*however* long that may be).

You will see a black steed, mounted by the image of a young lady in an old-fashioned dress. The duo will be in a furious hurry to get home, soon, to heal the long breech between father and daughter.

Of course, the strangest thing about this sight will be the young woman. For, you see, she hasn't any head at all.

14

The Southern Indiana "Wave"

U FO sightings, it would seem, are endemic to Indiana. Indeed, at one time, Indiana ranked (right behind Florida) number two of reported UFO cases nationwide.

It should come as no real surprise, then, that in 1987, the Mutual UFO Network of Indiana, or MUFON, as it is known nationwide, recorded a series of sightings that defy rational explanation, and give new credence to the high ranking visibility UFOs have in the Hoosier State.

An anonymous lady in Mauchport was out, early one evening, when her dog gave came forth with a series of terrified barks and utterances. Looking up, the woman was stunned to silence when she noted that, just above her, was a strange, domed-craft operating in a bizarre "falling leaf" fashion that is often reported in UFO cases.

The craft was perfectly circular, and gave forth no sound. The woman soon decided to hurry inside and phone for the neighbor, but suddenly noticed the bizarre vehicle began to ascend, as a ring of glowing lights unexpectedly flared around the rim of it.

It shot up and out of sight within moments. The witness' word was considered unimpeachable, and she stood nothing to gain by lying.

Strange glowing "balls of light" were likewise witnessed near Corydon, and even investigated by the police. These balls of light would bounce and spin, hover, blink on and off, and generally behave in such a strange manner that witnesses were beside themselves wondering what on earth they could possibly represent (they were not, obviously, of sufficient size or proportion to be actual vehicles). It was that same year (1987) that MUFON arranged for investigators to travel to the area, and witness for themselves. Although most of what they saw appeared to be nothing more than the landing lights of conventional aircraft, one of the investigators reportedly did see, independently, a glowing orb hovering during the episode.

One of the stranger aspects of the scenario involved one of the witnesses, and a police officer, following the glowing balls of light in the car, as if in attempt to capture or detain one. Whether their

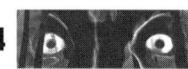

aspirations would have been entirely in vain or not is a matter of speculation, but what is for certain is that a duo of officers was so effected by the mysterious glowing orbs that they set up a vigil on one of the witnesses' property to catch a glimpse of them.

They were not disappointed.

Two glowing objects, each dipping up and down like yo-yos, and alternating luminosity and dimness (one would go dark while the other was lit up), appeared above a tree line in the distance, approximately "400-500 yards away." Neither of the objects ever made any sound.

Later, when checking on the status of aerial activity for the evening from neighboring Fort Knox, it proved apparent that there was nothing "unidentified" seen on radar, and no incoming flights (or anything else for that matter) that could have accounted for the strange visitation.

This visitation was reported by a Mr. Weronka to the *Louisville Courier Journal*.

Moving up and away from our glowing balls of light, we have the story of a farm boy, a stout-hearted all-American youth, who one Spring night in 1987, while working out in the fields of his farm near State Road 32, saw a strange object hovering over him while he was riding his tractor. Amazingly, the young man didn't immediately turn tail and run, but continued to hurriedly do his work, noting that it got "very bright" and that "I could see where I was going with no trouble. I could see the spreader and everything!"

He hurriedly went about finishing the final rows, with the large (it was described as being nearly the size of a house) object floating over his head. He then came out of the barn, after getting his brother, who both observed the pentagonal-shaped craft hovering within eighty feet of their grain silo. It alternated white, blue, and orange light, before rising into the air, and quickly zooming away. Both of the youths were described as dependable, hard-working, and without much imagination.

One of the officers involved in the "glowing balls of light" vigil went on, later that year, to have his own "close encounter" with a strange, "boomerang-shaped" vehicle he described as "huge." Coming off of Barren Road, ten miles or so from Corydon, he came over the hill and his high-beams hit an enormous object.

"It was shaped like a boomerang, and it was huge," he would later say. It was also only about a hundred feet off the roadway, although it quickly did a disappearing act. Next, it was directly above his truck, the lights having now turned to shimmering blue, and then it, likewise, zoomed away.

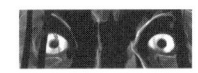

How's that for a special roadway surprise?

A "Mrs. K" was getting herself a drink of water at the kitchen sink one evening in August, when, suddenly, she spotted what appeared to be two strange, glowing balls of light dancing amidst the tree tops. As if that weren't enough, in a few moments they were joined by a black, disk-shaped object with a dome. A classic flying saucer.

This object ejected another light, which quickly joined the trio. The lights seemed to scan the environment over the surrounding trees for a moment, before being absorbed back into the black domed object, which then took off at an enormous velocity. Mrs. K was, altogether, rather shocked and embarrassed by her sighting, and likewise, stood nothing to gain by making up a hoax.

An anonymous man named "Jim" was driving along when he had a terrifying encounter with an object "as big as a good-sized car" that overtook him while driving down a country road. The object, which interfered with the radio and electrical operation of his vehicle, zipped over his vehicle, swerved to avoid hitting a car, and then swerved another way to avoid hitting a house. The object then proceeded upward, over some power lines, but Jim was able to get a good look at it.

He described is as a classic "flying saucer," with domes on top and bottom, and said that it glowed with an eerie greenish glow. Furthermore, he claimed that it was surrounded by lights around the rim, an amazing blue flash on top, and that it had a system of "weathervanes," or antenna-like objects issuing out of the top. Jim was known as a solid young man, attested to by both parents and friends, and was never have believed to have concocted the story.

An enormous UFO, one with the wings swept forward in a disturbing v-formation (like a 747 flying in reverse) was seen by two men in two different vehicles on December 17th, 1987. Both described a huge, slow-moving object with a red light in the center, surrounded by a mysterious "white floodlight." Both claimed the object made no sound whatsoever. Neither man had ever seen anything even remotely like it in the air before.

Of course, there are a plethora of other classic UFO sightings, and the ones we've mentioned so far have fallen into one of the three classic categories, Close Encounters of the First Kind (CE1), which is a sighting of an unidentifiable flying object in close proximity, where there is little or no doubt about the object of being of non-earthly origin.

For a Close Encounter of the Second Kind (CE2), the object must, in some way, interfere with the environment, or leave some other kind of calling-card (burn marks, bent or broken trees, radio or electrical

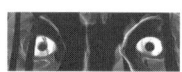

interference, fires, etc.) Such a case was reported in the *South Bend Tribune* in April of 2005 when the Indiana MUFON (Mutual UFO Network) met to conference over a strange series of sightings in Fulton County. The meeting, which took place in Rochester, was attended by the ten witnesses, everyone of which was more than eager to talk about the estrange disc-shaped craft they had seen. Interestingly, another attendee passed around pictures of an alleged "crop circle" that was found in Columbia City.

(Of course, we have not had occasion to touch upon this particular sort of phenomenon, but it is as bizarre as it is controversial. And, frequently, it follows UFO sightings as butter follows bread. A "crop circle" as most readers know, is a pictogram found pressed into a standing field of wheat, verging anywhere from simple circles to elaborate pictograms that defy any skeptic to explain how they could have possibly been made by pranksters. Alas, many crop circles HAVE turned out to be the work of pranksters, and some have even demonstrated how they managed, with a stick of wood, some string, and some flashlights, to fake the enormous pictograms by pressing down the wheat a they walked through the field at night.

And yet, the circles continue to appear, and some, perhaps legitimate anomalous crop formations have exhibited strange properties when analyzed, including a mutation of the grain itself, strange electromagnetic properties, an ability to throw off a compass or Geiger counter, etc. And, of course, they are often seen in open fields after UFOs have been sighted there. It's a phenomenon of, at best, tenuous relation, much like the "cattle mutilation" phenomenon, and it is also hard to come by reliable information as to which crop circles are hoaxes, and which are believed to be the authentic artifact. Hence, we have not thoroughly investigated it for the purposes of completing this volume.)

As stated earlier, UFO sightings are endemic to Indiana. And not just the first two types of Close Encounters, of course.

The next account has a factory worker who experienced that rarer of UFO sightings, the Close Encounter of the Third Kind, in which a UFO craft is seen either landed or in the air, and with the accompaniment of an occupant. The man describes how in 1967, a buddy called him out to the parking lot from his post at a factory to see an object that had suddenly appeared hovering in the air. Perplexed, and finding it difficult to see clearly due to the bright parking lot lights, he clearly saw enough to frighten and perplex him, as it would be decades (this was 1967) until he told the full story.

The object was circular, slow-moving, wobbled on its axis, and seemed to hover above without making a single sound. What was

more disturbing however, claimed the man, was the fact that he could clearly make out a row of solid windows, behind which he could see... figures, moving about in a sort of red haze.

One wonders who, or what, those figures represented.

———————————————

One additional folktale from the annals of Indiana UFO legendry seems oddly appropriate here, if only because it represents a classic case of *Walking A Lonely Road When Something Strange Happens*. Also, it is rather humorous, after a fashion.

An unidentified man, perhaps a poor transient, was walking down a country lane near Graysville in the middle of the night, when, suddenly, coming up over a field he saw a bright, silent light, that was steadily gaining speed toward him. Terrified, he seemed to be glued to the spot (a not uncommon occurrence) when the bright object came roaring (well, actually, perhaps it wasn't roaring—we simply use a figure of speech here) overhead, and shot a bright, intense ray of light down upon him, instantly knocking him out and scorching his skin badly.

When he awoke, he was in Sullivan Hospital, being treated for serious burns. He'd been advised by the doctors that, had the temperature not been so incredibly cold it necessitated the extra layers of clothing he had been wearing, he would almost certainly have fared far worse, possibly succumbing to fatal burns.

Lucky for him, I guess.

15

Jittery Jaunt:
Teleporting through the
Creepy Countryside

Since we are, if nothing else, creatures of habit, we found it quite necessary to revisit our previous volume, wherein we took the reader on an imaginary voyage through a dozen or more haunted Indiana locales—all the better to educate those seeking information on the creaking hollows and ghost-choked cemeteries of old Indiana.

First, let us draw the magic circle of protection about ourselves, making sure to say all the proper incantations and spells to ensure that, while our flight through the ether of the unknown may be a properly frightening one, it in no way endangers our safety. Then, let us summon forth, from the crumbling pages of so many august tomes, a few dreadful tidbits to whet the appetites of wonder-seekers everywhere.

Wolf Mansion

We begin our spectral voyage (after beating our way through the midnight hour traffic of so many fleeting phantoms) in the quiet town of Portage, where rears before us the stately, reverent visage of Wolf Mansion. The owner, a reported keeper of slaves, went mad one accursed night, and killed each of his slaves and their children. Later, in a fit of grief over what he had done, he finished off his own family with an axe, then put the barrel of a gun in his mouth. Legend has it that at times, you can see mysterious figures peeping from the windows, strange, garbed figures moving about on the property (and disappearing), and those that have been inside, swear that they have heard moans and groans, felt the clammy touch of spirit hands, and generally have a feeling that there are mysterious eyes upon them at all times.

It is also said that the tower (which formerly held a bell that was rung to call the slaves to attention) can still be heard to give forth with the

spectral ring of ages past, when the blood of slaves was spilled here by a man who had lost his mind.

Tippecanoe Place Restaurant

Next, we take you to South Bend, to sit for a mouth-watering morsel of a tale at the Tippecanoe Place Restaurant. Once the home of Studebaker scion Clement Studebaker, a man that made and lost a fortune, it is highly believed to be the location of his eventual suicide. Whatever the objective truth may be in that regard, the Studebaker mansion in South Bend is a place where the tragedy of the past meets the hopefulness of the living with a strange, resonant wail.

In the early part of the last century, the entire place erupted into a smoking inferno, killing a nanny and small child , and (apparently) leaving behind the grief and tragedy of a sort of psychic echo in its wake. Reports of cold spots, strange noises, haunting melodies trickling forth from the old ballroom, and the sensation of mysterious "eyes" being on you at all times, have been reported by a variety of anonymous witnesses. And don't worry about getting your drinks on time. The liquor bottles have been known to fly from their shelves on their own accord.

10ᵗʰ Street Bridge

From the posh interior of the Tippecanoe Place, we next travel to the humble burg of Gas City, in Grant County, where the 10th Street Bridge bears the unhappy spirit of a construction worker, who fell from the bridge to his death many years ago. Today it is said that on certain nights of the year you can see a figure clinging, desperately, at the edge of the bridge, with fingers that are eternally slipping on the rough edge toward a watery grave below. Also, it is said that powerful screams can be heard by those who cross the bridge and, we must assume, are equipped with the psychic sensitivity to hear them.

East Side School

We don't have to beam ourselves very far afield for a next stop, for Gas City is where the pleasant playground of the old East Side School still retains, reportedly, the shivery laughter and still-exuberant screams of playing children who are not there, at least, in bodily form. The educational stomping grounds for generations of this happy hamlet, the old East Side School apparently still retains a merry-go-round that spins, at times, of its own accord. Believe it if you will.

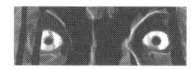

Indiana Repertory Theatre

Onward we fly, on spirited wings, toward Indianapolis, where the former owner of the Indiana Repertory Theatre is still busying himself worrying about his physical health, even though his physical body has long been laid to rest. Apparently, the man had been a fanatical physical fitness buff, and his incessant jogging between bouts of paperwork would continue on the upstairs mezzanine, particularly on days when the weather was inclement.

His exercise would prove to be a test in futility, however, for he was killed in an unfortunate automobile accident. Some would claim this ironic, given the nature of a man that spent so much time furiously moving his feet, but, whatever the case, one undeniable thing can be ascertained: he's still jogging the upstairs mezzanine of the theatre, to this very day.

Or so some would claim.

Devil's Hollow

From a jogging theatre owner to the bearer of a hooked hand and a "secret treasure," we take you now to Fort Wayne, to unfold one of the strangest sagas yet told in our torrid tome. This story may leave you feeling the clutches of a hooked claw rake across your neck after you get done reading it.

Supposedly, in a little-known area called "Devil's Hollow," there is an old house that was once occupied by a strange man and his long-suffering wife. The man had a hook where his right hand should have been, and he was rumored to have secret connections to Nazis in Germany, as well as knowing the whereabouts of a substantial portion of stolen Nazi treasure. Whether there was any truth to this legend or not can never, now, be fully ascertained, but what is certain is that the man was a violent, abusive drunk, who frequently beat his wife and terrorized local children into nicknaming him their "boogeyman."

They were not long, however, to enjoy the company of his (earthly) presence, for this mad individual one day went clean out of his skull, butchered his wife and child with an axe, and hung himself on a nearby bridge.

Strangely, before he enacted this atrocity, he completed the construction of a bizarre monument to his madness, a strange, irregularly built fence whose old boards crisscross up and down in unusual patterns. Some say that the very wise, or the very psychically gifted, can read the entire sordid saga of the man in the shapes and contours of this fence, and that it holds the secret to where his vast sums of gold are buried.

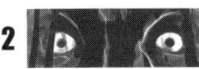

Of course, the hooked-handed Nazi is as eager to protect his gold, in death, as he was to protect it during his short, bitter existence. It is said that strange lights can be seen to play over the countryside near Devil's Hollow, and that if you go out to the house, alone, you will see the image of a man hanging as you try and cross the bridge. If you pass this grave sentinel without turning away in panic, then further along, in the dim reaches where the old house sits, you will see a light, burning eternally, in the old upstairs window. You may also see a presence in a hat and a long dark cloak. This image may reach out to strike at you, with one hooked hand slinging desperately at the air, in a futile attempt to guard a treasure that may never have existed at all.

These things may happen, but we wouldn't swear by them.

Satan's Church

Ah, onward we move, through the Infinite Void, now to Kokomo. Having visited the "Devil's Hollow" we now make for a pleasant stop at "Satan's Church," a boarded-up house of worship that no longer bears the redemptive touch of the Most High God. Rumor has it that the cemetery behind it is cursed by the apparitions of the walking dead, and that growling curses can be heard to erupt from the ground, and from inside the boarded-up confines of the church proper. Also, a pair of glowing eyes can be seen in the darkness, while glowing orbs and a "foul mist" cling like a sepulchral blanket to the edges of the place.

To top matters off, it is said that mysterious, underground "Satanic covens" have used the cemetery (and perhaps even the interior of the church?) as a place for the invocation of diabolical forces, no doubt during the most high holidays of *Walpurgisnacht,* or even Halloween.

Satanists or no, we wouldn't advise taking in Sunday services at "Satan's Church." It doesn't strike the present author as being very spiritually edifying (depending, of course, upon your respective religious persuasion).

Blood Road

From "Satan's Church" we next travel to "Blood Road" in Dunkirk, for the eerie tale of a maniacal farmer who murdered his barren wife. One night, after bashing in her skull, he placed her body in the back of his pickup truck; heading off down the darkened country lane, while he was driving, the body (which had, apparently, been tied-up in the bed of the truck, which had no tailgate), came unstuck, and nearly fell out the back. It was dragged, unknowingly, down miles of rough road, spurting a slick miasma of blood like a slug leaving slime in its wake.

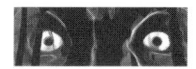

It is said that travelers of Blood Road can see this ectoplasm trail of grue to this very day, as they drive along at night. That would be enough to frighten anyone to stay away. But wait! There's even more.

According to some accounts, the homicidal farmer butchered his small son, as well. It is said that the apparition of the tot can be seen beckoning, at times, from the side of the road, lonely and lost; looking for the love, perhaps, he was ever denied during his short existence.

Northside High School

Next, we come to the (seeming) relative safety of a bustling Indiana high school (although, how safe any school can be considered in this day and age of random shootings is a matter of debate) , in particular Northside High School in Fort Wayne.

Once the site of an Indian burial plot, the land itself was reportedly cursed by the ancient Chieftain who refused to ever allow anything to be built upon it. Of course, his warning went unheeded. The high school itself has been the scene of ghostly visitations, including that of a teen-aged girl, who reportedly has been sighted in the gymnasium, walking through the halls after hours, and can be heard whispering to herself in the cafeteria.

A janitor (who suffered a massive heart attack and dropped dead at work) is reportedly still on the job, and a construction worker who was killed in a building renovation has been seen to haunt the auditorium. A construction crew hired in the early nineties for some major work re-portedly had laborers who quit, or refused to be in the building alone. It would appear that, as far as the ghosts of Northside High School are concerned, class is always in session.

The Chief's Son

The Potawatomi Indians believed that the St. Joseph River (which they called Sauk-wauk-sil-buck, later Sau-was-see-bee) was a dual river, one a flowing beauty that supplied them with fish, and which they could float their canoes down river, to trade with settlers and friendly tribes, the other a vast underground stream flowing into the Underworld.

One such story has the Chief of the Potawatomi, who, out of all his children, loved his little son the most. Yet, tragically, the River Spirit (who had an ironic, if not particularly large appetite) saw in the boy something that It fancied, too. The Chief's son went down to the river to play, and was never seen again.

The chief, who nearly mourned himself to death, spent the remainder of his days looking for the lost tot, but, finding it fruitless, he simply sat

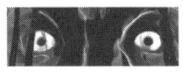

one cold winter's day on the banks of the St. Joseph, leaned against a tree, and froze to death. A sort of passive-aggressive suicide.

Of course, a school rests on the exact spot now, and it is said by employees that they have caught a glimpse, at odd and sundry times, of the image of a Native American chief can be seen roaming the hallways, perhaps continuing his fruitless search for his little boy, into eternity.

Mysterious Lights

We are still whipping through the crawling chaos of clinging mist towards a new destination, that being: Francesville. There, a mysterious light can be seen skimming through a cornfield. Legend reputes that two brothers long ago were riding in a carriage, when the other brother managed, through misadventure, to fall out, being horribly decapitated under the wheels in the process. The light seen is supposedly that of his brother, who combs the tall crops in search of the messy remains of the head, so it could be properly buried.

Hostess House

Across the street from where I presently live is an old house called Hostess House, a rather stately-looking old place considering the down-at-the-heels condition of most of the rest of the surrounding neighborhood. The house, which serves as a "social showpiece," now houses restaurants and shops. It also has a reputation for housing the resident spirit of a murdered woman who was killed long ago.

The man who perpetrated the murder, incidentally, was a distant relative of an individual known to the present author, so the details leading up to this particular crime were well-known to him.

The crime was perpetrated by his cousin, a young man who hailed from the mean streets of Chicago. He had gotten mixed-up, at a rather young age, in the seedy world of drugs and gangs, and his relatives, having become concerned for his safety, and seeking to get him to "clean his act up," had sent him to his relatives in Marion.

At the time, Marion, Indiana, was an altogether cleaner, nicer, and thoroughly more law-abiding place than what it, unfortunately has evolved into since. Of course, many communities now, regrettably, are plagued by gangs, crime, drugs, and the specter of social decay. It was not so pronounced even thirty years ago. But, I digress.

The young man, in point of fact, did not "clean up his act," although he might have done so for a short time. One fateful evening, he made his way downtown, perhaps finally "fed to the teeth" with being so "good" for so long, to celebrate his "coming of age" at a local bar.

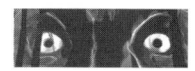

His celebration was to be short-lived.

Drunk as the proverbial skunk, he walked (or was rather, ejected) from the bar in an intensely intoxicated, drugged, and paranoid state. Walking the streets in the wee hours of the morning, inebriated, is never a good idea for those who wish to remain on the right side of the law so, knowing full well he might be picked up, he stumbled upon the grounds of the Hostess House, perhaps imagining the stately old place was so large no one would notice if he snuck in, found a silent nook in which he could dry out, or wait until dawn.

Alternately, it has been suggested that he broke into the Hostess House with the idea of robbery in mind. It could have been a desire to buy drugs which drove him there that fateful early morning, but, whatever it was, somehow he managed to climb (precariously we must assume, considering his drunken state plus the height of the building itself), to an open window and creep inside.

It must have been very dark, and although we won't linger long over the unmerry details of the ensuing event, suffice it to say he was not alone in the building. An elderly lady discovered the young lout roaming around upstairs, drunk and out of his mind.

She may have screamed, or she may have boldly demanded what he was doing there, and threatened to call the police. At the mention of the word "police," the young man may have flown into a rage. At any rate, reportedly he grabbed a blunt object, perhaps a table lamp, and proceeded to bludgeon the elderly woman to death.

The details to what happened next, as they were presented to this author, are a little unclear, but suffice it to say that the young man was apprehended in a short amount of time, having left a trail of bloody evidence in his wake. He was tried, convicted, and sent to prison where he, undoubtedly, belonged. However, that is not the end of the story.

It is said that on moonlight nights the ghost of the old woman can be seen standing on the balcony outside, staring off into the darkness below. (Perhaps wondering at all the new, sporty cars and loud, thumping music erupting out of them?)

We have passed this particular abode on many occasions, and have yet to see a trace of her, all though we will concede that the place itself, which is lit heavily, eerily, in front, but recedes to darkness in the back, does have its own unnerving, foreboding quality. We've not yet been inside, and we're not sure we ever want to go…

Boots Street

While we are stopped in Marion, we might as well take a little tour through the once-auspicious residence of a family that lived in a glorious

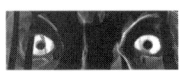

old Victorian on Boots Street, a neighborhood that has, sadly, fallen the way of so much of the rest of this once-pleasant Hoosier burg. It is a tale retold by Mark Marimen in his excellent book *Haunted Indiana 2,* and recounts the childhood memories of a woman who grew up in a house that she claimed was malevolently haunted.

One of her earliest memories is of experiencing a general feeling that there was something "not quite right" about the environment in which she was growing up. One of the worst aspects of the whole house for her was descending the old oaken staircase, which was lit only by a single light from a drawstring above (which, being a youngster, she could of course not reach). "Marie Dudeck" explains that she often felt a sense of fearful presence when descending this particular staircase in the dark. Even as a child, "Marie Dudeck" explains to Marimen, "…I remember feeling the cold and knowing I was not alone on those stairs. It was a frightening, threatening feeling."

As well it should be. "Marie" recounts her father, one night, very carefully closing the closet door in his bedroom, with a worried expression on his face. He explained that one night, just before settling down to sleep, he had forgotten and left the closet door wide open. He had drifted off to troubled slumber when, at an ungodly hour of the morning, something stirred him to wakefulness.

He was stunned and horrified to see the dark apparition of a woman emerge from the closet, her finger pointing out, meaninglessly, in front of her, as if she were staring at something in the distance. Whatever it was, he couldn't guess, but "Marie" was certain it was a story her father hadn't made up just to try and amuse or frighten the kids. She tells Marimen, "Dad obviously believed it and he repeated this story to us often."

It was not to be the only manifestation of a ghostly presence in the unidentified old house on Boots Street (which, truth be told, is rather rife with crumbling old houses). In time, several older aunts finally moved out (perhaps to nursing care?), and the family now found themselves the sole owner of the old place. The girls, "Marie" and her sister, were moved to a disused downstairs room that was converted into a bedroom. It had formerly been servants quarters during the bygone era of opulence when such arrangements were commonplace.

Much to the chagrin of her mother, she often swore she could hear "Marie" walking about downstairs at all hours of the night. When confronted with this, or when angrily asked to "Get back in bed and go to sleep!" an awakened Marie could often be counted on to come to her bedroom door and confess that she had been in bed the whole time. Apparently, someone was making footsteps, often, all night downstairs. Whoever it was though, it was not one of the girls.

The most terrifying incident, however, happened not to Marie, but to her sister, who, while going to the bathroom one night, saw something in the parlor that caused her to let out peals of screaming fright, waking up the entire family.

Apparently, downstairs, the way to the bathroom led past the empty, darkened parlor. Cheery enough by day, but at night, when suddenly the hustle and bustle of living energy has reached a low ebb…it could have as sinister and unwelcoming a feeling as the rest of the sleeping home.

The sister (who took much time and coaxing to calm down) swore that, as she was walking down the darkened hallway to the bathroom, she looked over in the parlor. Sitting in the parlor was the figure of a woman dressed in black.

We take it such an intruder would be enough to unnerve even the boldest among us. To the young girl, it might have seemed as if hell itself had flung open a gate and let loose a revenant.

Strange figures and phantom footsteps soon led the family to realize they were sharing their domestic tranquility (or, perhaps, lack thereof) with a very special guest. It wasn't until sometime later that the pieces of the puzzle began to fit together for Marie, but not until she discovered a hidden interest in genealogy.

She began to consult the elderly aunts about the history of the family, and she got quite an earful. She could name all of her most distant relatives in time, but she kept zeroing back to the issue of the family house, and the history of who had lived and, most assuredly, died there.

One name that was mentioned was "Great Aunt Margery," but it was a name without many details attached to it, and Marie's elderly relatives refused to elaborate. It would not be until next summer, while, when visiting some more distant cousins in Florida, Marie would finally begin to unravel the tragic history of the house and the woman who had died in the very bedroom in which she now slept.

Although at first reluctant to open an particularly aged and corroded can of worms, an elderly relative (described as being very "forthright") confessed that Great Aunt Margery had died of "peritonitis" while screaming in an agony of pain and fury in the back bedroom of the old house. She delivered, perhaps ominously, imprecations to God, begging his forgiveness, but knowing he could never forgive her for all the evil she had enacted in her short, bitter life.

And to what, pray tell, was she referring?

It may seem strange to us in the present era of loose mores and non-traditional virtue, but at one time the idea of a young, unmarried woman becoming pregnant was considered a moral and social blight from which virtually nothing could redeem the transgressor. Margery, having slept with a married man, had made it all doubly worse, and was now caught in the middle

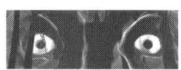

of something she was not, in any way, prepared to deal with at her tender age. She made a decision that was both rash, and in those days, illegal.

It would also prove fatal.

She procured the services of a quack abortionist, a man whose name is lost to this record, but who must have been sorely qualified to endeavor the particular medical task he was entrusted to perform. We do not have any record of how much he was paid. If it was even a pittance, it was far too much.

Somehow, the operation was botched, and Margery grew gravely ill. She was put, like a dirty secret in the disused back bedroom, and tended to as best the family were able. However, it soon became apparent that there was little chance for her recovery, and funeral preparations must have been hastily drawn up.

She raged and ranted, as we mentioned before, begging the forgiveness of God. Whether or not she found it is a matter of strict conjecture. Depending on what one, personally, believes concerning the possible nature of ghostly manifestations, the answer could very well be…no.

Marie (who must have returned home with her head swimming of images on the "old days," and not a little bit of unsettled fear mixed with curiosity), settled down along with her sister in the room one night, trying, as best she could, to relax to a troubled sleep.

She was not long to remain confined to the realm of portents and uneasy dreams, for, in due time, she felt a coldness steal over her, even in her sleep, and she awoke to a sight she would never forget, again, for the rest of her life.

Standing before her, dressed in a flowing, black, Victorian gown, was the apparition of a cadaverous woman. Marie was paralyzed with fear (a common enough occurrence, actually, during such "bedroom visitations" whatever they look like or however they present themselves). She closed her eyes tightly, bit her lip, trying to make doubly sure that this wasn't the residual image of a half-remembered nightmare. No dice. She opened her eyes, and the ghost was still there, staring off into a space beyond—beyond anything any of us could imagine, possibly.

Then she vanished…as quickly as she had come.

That was the last, most terrifying encounter Marie had with "Great Aunt Margery," but it was not the end of the manifestations of Margery. The strange footsteps often continued, long into the night, and the feeling of the "presence" of a cold, angry, lonely woman who was trapped persisted, in a metaphysical sense, in a kind of locked groove of being from which she could not escape—perhaps she was looking for a way out, and couldn't find it. Perhaps she is looking still.

Marie told Marimen that, years later, she returned to the house to take pictures of the outside. It had long ago been sold to a landlord, who

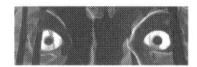

had converted it into upstairs and downstairs apartments. Curiously, he was never able to rent out the upstairs.

He related an amusing story, while confiding that the house seemed "funny" somehow. The tenant in the downstairs apartment one day called him, asking him why he had not been informed that the upstairs rooms had been rented. He assured the troubled tenant that, indeed, they had not. This distinctly troubled the man, as he had been subject to loud footsteps echoing from the empty rooms upstairs, many, many nights in a row now.

Marie relates to Marimen that she believes that, just because the ownership of the house had changed, did not mean that Margery was going to "move on" or quit her frequent, troubled perambulations.

"It was her house, and she was everywhere in it. It was not a pleasant thing at all," Marie said.

The Haunted House

For our last spinetingler on the terror-trail, as the moon dips low and the first, chilly, ghastly rays of the hated daylight peep just above the horizon, we must turn back the clock to a tale of wild ghostliness the likes of which may leave the reader stone mad with horror. Or, at the very least, leave them feeling cold as a stone.

We make no promises or apologies, one way or the other.

Our scene can be set thusly: Mr. William S. Lingle, Editor of the Lafayette *Evening Courier*, played host and bon-vivant to a number of distinguished men one evening in 1872, including Judge J.K. Higginbotham, and a "Professor Amos Dillington" of a distinguished university. Two other men were reported as being present, both of them minor newspapermen from elsewhere in the state. It was the middle of June.

After dinner, the men must have repaired to the "gentleman's smoking room" for a few cigars and perhaps a few glasses of brandy. The subject, for some unfathomable reason, turned to the supernatural, and Professor Dillington confessed himself quite an enthusiast on this particular subject. Lingle, feeling perhaps mischievous as well as adventurous, suggested an outing to a house he knew of that was, reputedly, haunted. It was a two-room house, much fallen to ruin, with no upstairs and a dirt floor. It was around a mile outside Lafayette city limits, and without much further goading, the men were convinced to take off in separate carriages at around nine that evening, finally following Lingle's coach to the dilapidated old place.

Upon their arrival, they looked over the house carefully, noting the boarded-up windows and the general air of disrepute and decay which hung about the mournful old dwelling. Choking back the dust behind hands holding kerchiefs and shivering with a little chill (and a little fright,

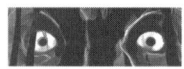

perhaps?) the men settled themselves on the scant, moldy furniture, and waited,. They had not long to sit.

In a short time, according to the account published by Mr. Lingle in the pages of the *Evening Courier* (and reported later in the excellent book *Hoosier Hauntings* by K.T. MacRorie), a strange, smoky light began to play in the darkness, and several men had to lean over, adjusting their spectacles to make sure that they weren't hallucinating in the moonlit dark. The light grew to a strange, dancing, luminescent fire, and began to metamorphose into the form of a great white wolf, who seemed to be running in mid-air. He then stopped, as if exhausted, and the swimming mist (or ectoplasm) from which he was formed began to swirl and change again, until it was now something quite hideous and bizarre to behold.

It was a creature not unlike a large frog, with the jaws of an alligator, and sporting a tail like a kangaroo. Very loathsome, indeed, and it floated in mid-air for what seemed several minutes, much to the amazement of the assembled.

Then, yet again, the cloud of ectoplasm shifted, until, finally, it took the form of a Native American warrior, holding a tomahawk and a torch. This strange figure stood, seemingly amazed himself at his condition, before turning, running into the darkness, and disappearing into a solid wall.

The men suddenly broke into a tumult of confused wonderment and fright, and it was everything Mr. Lingle could do to calm the terrified company and get everyone back to their rightful senses. Professor Dillington, who suddenly confessed to being a "learned practitioner" of the occult, decided that they should return later that night (or at least, all those willing to return should do so), and that he would endeavor to contact this bizarre spirit, and henceforth see what the fellow was all about.

Professor Dillington (who carried his very own "magic wand," it turned out, in a leather carrying case), followed the men back to the abandoned haunt. Going inside and still choking from the darkened dust, he proceeded to draw a circle with his wand on the dirt floor, dividing the circle with various forty-five degree angles and inscribing therein a series of cryptic runes, Enochian writing, or perhaps regular old Hebrew lettering.

He therein placed a tripod and lamp with a strange burning sort of oil inside the circle, and the astounded men settled down once more to wait and see what would transpire.

In the stinking smoke and light of the lamp, the ghostly image of the Native began to slowly appear. Professor Dillington (apparently an old hand at spiritualistic séances), began to speak with the spirit confidently, asking it why it was too disturbed to move on, to the "Happy Hunting Ground."

The Native warrior, who spoke in a combination of French and English, answered that it was the spades and shovels of the settlers, the building of a city that was growing exponentially, which had disturbed his slumber. Apparently, his remains had been disturbed, the land was hallowed, and had been desecrated by the new development that was going on. "White Wolf" (which was how he identified himself) was not at all pleased by this.

On his arm, incidentally, was a tattoo of the strange creature he had metamorphosed into before: the frog-like creature with alligator jaws. When asked about this, he explained that this particular Slithery Something had once existed in vast numbers in the lakes and swamps of the land, but had long since gone extinct.

"White Wolf," whose remains were buried in the Longlois reservation northeast of Lafayette, spoke for a little while longer, but he grew increasingly weak, and finally faded from sight. As to what could be done to preserve his disturbed remains, the men had not a clue, but the story of their strange encounter was much read and discussed by readers of the Lafayette *Evening Standard* for quite some time, until the events themselves took on the auspices of a local legend.

One young man even claimed to speak (in spiritualist séances) with the spirit of White Wolf, and claimed that he could not rest until a fence was built around Spring Vale Cemetery. Apparently, though, the young man was not much believed.

As to the location of the old house, although we wouldn't advise our readers to go poking around anyplace they are not welcome (by man or… otherwise), reportedly it now rests possibly east of Murdock Park, in the vicinity of the ironically named Sunnyside Junior High in Lafayette.

As for White Wolf himself, who knows? Did he find peace, and move onward? Only God could say for certain.

However, our personal "jittery jaunt" has now taken us through the halls of night, the forests of fantasy, and memory, and history, onto the shores of time, and left us all the better for having toured the dust-shrouded corridors of Haunted Hoosier History. Time to shuffle on our "mortal coils," and walk the world as men, in daylight, once more.

Haunted Hoosier History…

Hey, that's not a bad title, is it?

16

Searching for Amelia

The life and death of Amelia Earhart was a mystery wrapped in an enigma.

The Aviatrix, who mysteriously flew into a cloud bank to never again be seen, has been the subject of much speculation and controversy over the years. And little wonder: During her lifetime, Amelia distinguished herself in the then male-dominated world of aviation, being the first woman to fly across the Atlantic, and intended to be the first woman to actually circle the world in an airplane before her mysterious final vanishing act.

Alas, Amelia made history for being The Woman Who Was Not There. Apparently, that peculiar fame has followed her in death.

Amelia Earhart was born in Archison, Kansas, on July 24, 1897. By all accounts she was a natural-born "tomboy" with no end to a love of climbing trees, riding horses, building forts, and talking with her friend "Pudgy." But it was the swirling, limitless skies that always entranced Amelia Earhart the most, and it was in the skies that her fate would eventually lay.

Amelia Earhart's dreams lay, literally, in the clouds. The fairly new sport of aviation, at that time still a frontier ready-made for square-jawed pioneers of the sky to barnstorm to new heights, and go for new distances and speeds, beckoned to Amelia like a prop-driven siren song from her earliest days. Of course, at the time, a woman's place was deemed to be, chiefly, in the kitchen, not in the airspace, and so Amelia found herself, often, bumping up against the male-dominated world of aviation like an angry bull determined to best a particularly noxious matador.

She would not be deterred by the prevailing sexist attitudes of the age. When Charles A. Lindbergh, a bonafide American hero, managed to become the first man to cross the Atlantic in an airplane, the entire country christened him a Living Legend (a role that, regrettably, would diminish in years, with his opposition to America's entry into the Second World War). Amelia must have known, somewhere deep inside herself, that one day she must follow in his giant footsteps. Since Lucky Lindy's Transatlantic triumph, fourteen other pilots, each trying to duplicate Lindbergh's flying feat, had gone to a watery grave.

Amelia, while working in a military hospital as a Red Cross nurse, thrilled to the stories of derring-do delivered to her by injured and ailing military pilots, all of them male. At the same time, she was attending aerial barnstorming expositions, thrilling to the wonder of (some might say suicidal) stuntmen quite willing to climb out on the wings of their bi-planes and swoop over roaring crowds to breathless acclaim.

She finally moved with her family from Massachusetts to Los Angeles, taking a job as a telephone operator, but her heart was still in the air, and she finally took the initial step that would seal her fate and place in history, forever. She signed up for local flying lessons, at first being met with some amount of skepticism and resistance by the male veterans at the airfield. She didn't let it faze her, and the skepticism on the part of her male colleagues slowly turned to respect and then to outright admiration, as Amelia turned out to not only be a competent pilot, but a veritable aeronautical genius in the making.

She not only knew how to fly, she knew her airplane on the inside, as well as the out, learning all she could about mechanics, instrument flying, etc. She became the first woman to soar to over 14,000 feet, and the first woman to accompany a pilot across the Atlantic— and live to tell the tale. When her parents divorced (forcing Amelia to sell her plane) she moved to Medford, Massachusetts, with her mother, taking employment as a social worker, and becoming a beloved friend to immigrant children, most of whom could not speak English. Some people, it would seem, are just naturally talented and good, from the inside out. This author feels Amelia Earhart was just such a person.

The Icarus-like lure of flight still beckoned, however, and Amelia was a regular and much-valued member of the aeronautical societies. She took every opportunity possible to become airborne, and still the dream of being the greatest woman pilot to ever crank a prop burned deeply within her breast.

It would soon be realized, beyond her wildest and most dangerous dreams.

Some of Amelia's feats included setting the first women's airspeed record of 181.8 miles per hour, competing in the first all-female air derby, taking a record-braking flight in a "gyroscope" (a primitive forerunner to the helicopter), and being instrumental in establishing passenger flight between New York, Washington, and Philadelphia. All this, and she found the time to be president of the first women's aeronautical association, and write a column for the fledgling *Cosmopolitan* (a column on aviation, of course).

With all of this going on, it is a little surprising that Amelia (who one imagines as being a sort of female aerial maverick happier behind an instrument panel than anywhere else), managed to fall in love with George Putnam, and was duly married. Putnam would be both husband, manager, mentor, and friend over the ensuing years, and one must imagine, with a sort of hopeless poignancy, how deeply he would feel the tragedy that occurred later.

Amelia, not satisfied with simply being the Most Famous Female Pilot in America, soon set her sights on the most dangerous (at the time) undertaking any pilot could contemplate at the time: the often-fatal Transatlantic flight. Alone.

It was a precarious ordeal, a true odyssey of hit-and-miss and near disaster that is quite beyond the scope of the present volume to adequately cover, but, needless to say Amelia survived the voyage.

On May 20th, 1932, Amelia Earhart landed in Londonberry, Scotland, and won instantaneous international acclaim. Now, not only was she a celebrity, she had flown across the Atlantic and landed directly in the pages of world history: She was the first woman to have ever made that voyage, and for it she was awarded France's Cross of the Legion of Honor, as well as the National Geographic Society's Gold Medal. She continued to set records, and was catapulted into the status of celebrity lecturer and role model to a new, more independent-minded sort of young woman, who saw in the fulfillment of Amelia's strange vision of aerial fame the promise that ANY dream, no matter the obstacles involved, could be attained with sufficient courage and effort.

When Amelia addressed a conference in New York concerning "Women Changing the World," in 1935, among those in attendance were Dr. Edward C. Elliot, president of Purdue University, who found himself very impressed with the dauntless courage of this remarkable young woman, and who later invited her and her husband to a dinner invitation, and the announcement of a special offer.

"We want you at Purdue," he stated flatly. Dr. Elliot, a progressive educator interested (coincidentally) in both aviation and the role of women in higher education and an advanced society, must have seen in Amelia the answer to a dream come true. Delighted, Amelia accepted unconditionally, although she did wonder what the nature of her duties, specifically, would be.

Amelia Earhart was made an honorary faculty member of Purdue University, an advisor to the Women's Career Department as well as the Aeronautics Department. This horrified some of the more ortho-

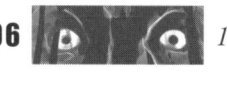

dox faculty members, who noted she was far from being "academically qualified" to be a faculty member. But her presence at Purdue was more in the order of boosting morale, anyway, and while she did lecture, her duties were chiefly to simply interact with the female students, to speak with them, and help inspire them. Which, many attested later, is exactly what she did.

(It certainly did rankle some staid, conservative Midwesterners, however, that Amelia had the temerity to keep such "scandalous" personal habits as wearing men's pants and being seen unchaperoned at local soda fountains, according to the excellent book *Haunted Indiana 2*.)

Amelia did not stint in her rigorous personal habits, and, while fulfilling duties at Purdue, kept up her steady schedule of lectures, writings, and interviews, as well as keeping a practiced hand behind the instrument panel. It was only a short time later that she began to contemplate the final, fatal adventure, for which she would forever become an enigma.

It was an around-the-world flight, a feat that had already been accomplished, but Amelia would, upon completion of this last, most dangerous deed, bring to the feat one important distinction: She would be the first woman to have ever accomplished it.

Secondly, though, she would also be the first to follow a path around the equator, the longest path. Doubly dangerous. Perhaps, at this stage, her overconfidence was getting the best of her.

It was a discussion of her plans with Dr. Elliot that led to the establishment of the "Amelia Earhart Fund for Aeronautical Research," and it was generous grants by the local elite that bought her the state-of-the-art plane in which she was to make the endeavor. Housed at the Purdue University hangar, the plane was a subject of continuous examination and tinkering by Amelia in the lead-up to her historic endeavor. In fact, for a shore period, she practically "haunted" the place.

She would fly from Oakland, California to Honolulu, she reckoned, and from there, across the equator until she arrived back in Oakland. Her navigator would be the ill-starred Fred Noonan; a man history would have trouble remembering considering his loss was virtually blotted out by the long shadow cast from Amelia.

The first attempt out was a disaster, and they survived the crash of their plane in Honolulu, limping back to California, for repairs and a few more months of waiting. Amelia seemed undaunted, despite the ill-omen.

Finally, in June of 1937, they set out on the second attempt, heading first to Miami, and then spending the next three weeks making

a dizzying itinerary of stops: San Juan, Dakar, Calcutta, and Papua, New Guinea.

They hoped to arrive back in California by the Fourth of July.

On July 2nd, they took off from New Guinea, heading for Howland Island. It was then as if the sky swallowed them up. It was the last time either one of them were ever heard from.

Though authorities mounted a relentless search (the most massive search for a vanished plane up till that point in history, in fact), it proved to be of no avail. Amelia Earhart, her co-pilot, and plane had vanished as mysteriously as if they flown directly into another dimension. In fact, in loonier circles of speculation, this is exactly what some individuals have suggested happened.

Also, UFOs have, of course, been blamed. A more conventional explanation might have Earhart crashing on a remote island, being killed, or surviving to be killed by the natives, or dying of natural causes. No one, I'm sure, will ever know the truth.

Some people are simply too good, too talented, too wonderful to remain long in this world. We are sure Amelia was one of them.

However, there are those at Purdue University that feel that, strictly speaking, something of Amelia remains behind at her once-

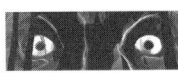

beloved adopted university. Stories have circulated for years that Amelia, though she be long dead and gone, has returned to walk the Spartan halls of her former residence hall, perhaps curious and confused at all the modern changes that have been wrought since her strange disappearance. Perhaps, though, she is delighted by them.

Stories from the mechanics that have worked at the Purdue Airport have related the tale of a shadowy female phantom that lurks in a corner of Hangar Number One, watching attentively everything that goes on. If approached, this female flier, a short woman dressed in a flight suit with close cropped hair (exactly the description of Amelia) seems to simply vanish. This account has been repeated a number of times from various sources.

An amusing anecdote has the WW2 Era military occupying the hangar to test out a super secret form of aircraft fuel—Sentries were stationed around Hangar 1, and the regular mechanics (who had, by now, become more than familiar with the ghost of the vanished Aviatrix) waited curiously to see if the extra presence of the military officials and soldiers would have any additional effect on the "ghost."

Indeed, they did not have long to wait. Late one night, they rushed out of the hangar at the sound of a soldier firing his rifle. White as the proverbial sheet, the man was yelling excitedly into his

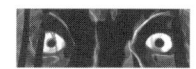

walkie-talkie, and soon a cadre of officers had assembled to debrief the sentry. His claim? That a strange "intruder," a short woman in a flight suit, had approached him in the night. When he ordered her to "halt!" she ignored him and kept coming. Hence, he shot.

Only the mechanics had any inkling of what the hubbub was really all about, and reportedly tried to explain, as best they could that, several years earlier, Hangar 1 had housed the plane Earhart had personally labored over for many long months. The plane that she, most likely, died in.

There is no record as to whether or not the officers bought the tale about Earhart's ghost, but we can well imagine they were not entirely amused by the episode.

More recently, a woman working in the Hangar office reported the sound of an old-fashioned prop engine being started up while she was sitting at her desk.

And it is not just Hangar 1 that is said to be haunted by Amelia, but her old residence hall, toward the "end room of the first floor," where she had stayed during her tenure as a "faculty member," is also said to be haunted by the strange form of a woman in old-fashioned clothing. The figure is of a woman with close-cut hair, who, upon being approached, is said to vanish into the surroundings. Also, at times, it is reported that the sounds of an old-fashioned typewriter can be heard late in the night, reportedly when Earhart was most fond of doing her writing.

Furthermore, doors and windows have reportedly opened and closed by themselves, and objects have a curious way of disappearing and reappearing in the strangest places. Is it the ghost of Amelia? Or, is it perhaps some other restless spirit?

Whatever the case may be, we can be sure of one thing: Amelia Earhart left her mark on Purdue University, and it is there that her spirit still, obviously, is strongly felt. In both the figurative, and perhaps even, literal sense.

17

Strangest Sons

In keeping with the tradition of our previous volume, we endeavor to present here some of the Hoosier State's more occult personages. In the former volume, we introduced you to Harold Sherman, a one-time writer for the Marion, Indiana, *Chronicle Tribune* who went on to become a full-time writer on psychic phenomena and the unexplained.

Of course, the scope of the present volume is quite a bit larger than that of simple ghosts, so we have dug through our files (which exude a faint whiff of sulphur) and retrieved the history of one William Dudley Pelley of Noblesville, who bore the distinction of not only being one of the leading American Nazis before World War II, but also the channel of otherworld entities that he took dictation for.

Pelley, who grew up in extreme poverty, spent his life struggling to become the best writer that he possibly could. He started to win great acclaim in the early part of the last century, eventually traveling to Hollywood where he churned out scripts for films. However, he soon became disillusioned with the jet-set lifestyle.

The reason? He had had a "near-death experience" which had completely changed his perception of reality, and forced him into a deep, concentrated study of metaphysics.

After setting out on a world-tour, Pelley acted as correspondent for a newspaper during the Bolshevik Revolution of 1917, witnessing many atrocities that were committed by the revolutionaries, and thereby gaining a lifelong hatred of Communism. It was this hatred, plus a growing anti-Semitism possibly gleaned from his traveling in Eastern Europe, that was to alter the course of his life for many years to come.

Upon returning to the States, Pelley founded several organizations, but among them was the Silver Legion, or the "Silver Shirts" as they were more popularly known, an anti-Semitic, pro-Nazi organization that was the pseudo-mystical counterpart to the German American Bund of imprisoned fascist Fritz Kuhn. Under the banner of the Silver Legion, Pelley published a plethora of magazines and pamphlets extolling the virtues of isolationism, *Mein Kampf*, National Socialist Germany, and, of course, paranoid anti-Semitic bigotry.

At the same time, he began to explore the outer reaches of various mystical experiences, including supposed contact with "entities" that existed on a "higher plane" of consciousness. Of course, this connection between fascism and the occult is nothing new[5]. Anton LaVey, the diabolical priest who founded the Church of Satan and authored *The Satanic Bible*, often hinted darkly of a "black order" of Satanists that existed during Germany's Weimar Era leading up to the Third Reich, and went so far as to suggest that an uncle serving in an administrative capacity in occupied Berlin had managed to smuggle forbidden Nazi movies back to the U.S., and that these films were full of Satanic and occult rituals and imagery. LaVey claimed that the rituals and imagery of these films influenced him a great deal as a young man.

Whatever the case as far as Nazism and the occult are concerned, Pelley's fascist activities and constant screeching against Roosevelt got him into hot water, particularly after the outbreak of war. Pelley soon found himself imprisoned on a fifteen-year sentence for sedition. He was paroled (some would say sadly) in 1950.

Pelley made sure to steer clear of controversial politics for the rest of his life, but he never lost his appetite for the weird. Upon release, he founded *Soulcraft* in Noblesville, as a publishing arm for a cult centered upon his communication with what he called "Star Guests" in one of his many books.

During the "Contactee" craze of the fifties, when little old ladies were busying themselves being whisked aboard "flying saucers" by tall, blond-haired (often) Venusian "Space Brothers" (who never failed to mouth the same New Age platitudes concerning the dangers of nuclear energy, environmental destruction, and the coming of Armageddon), Pelley struck up a friendship with California's George Adamski, a man whose claims of extraterrestrial visitation were met with cheers from True Believers, and jeers from the less completely credulous.

Adamski told a tale (complete with obviously phony photographs) of being directed to the high desert to meet with the tall, blond, completely human-looking occupants of a UFO "scout ship." Adamski claimed that his contact, "Orthon," had come to Earth to promote peace. Likewise, he claimed to have been taken aboard the ship, flown to a city on the moon, and to have received a special audience with the Pope. In short: Adamski's word was, at best, unreliable.

Of course, UFO contact tales are filled with such absurd claims, and one could posit (in much the same way that John Keel does in his Fortean classic *The Mothman Prophecies*) that those who experience UFO contact themselves are being "completely truthful," but that it is the *entities themselves* who create such wild hallucinations and tell outright fabrications. Whatever the case may be, Adamski fit well into the Pelley worldview, although it is not known if Pelley himself ever boarded a scout ship (we can find no mention of him having outright claimed to).

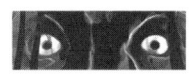

Pelley seems to have been only *telepathically* linked to the "Star Guests," who poured forth a seemingly endless stream of information and wisdom teachings for Mr. Pelley to convey to the world. (It is interesting to note, too, that Mr. Pelley's understudy at *Soulcraft*, at the time, was George Hunt Williamson, author of *Other Tongues-Other Flesh*, an exhaustive pseudo-mystical mishmash of UFO lore, ancient mythology, Biblical study, occult conjecture, and revisionist archaeology that would predate the "ancient astronaut" craze kicked off by Erich Von Daniken only two decades later.)

Jacques Vallee, the brilliant UFO researcher and occult theorist who authored the book *Messengers of Deception*, reveals the connections between Pelley, Adamski, Williamson, and other UFO Contactees, and postulates that the entire phenomenon is based around a secret (supernatural?) conspiracy to, perhaps, usher in the sort of fascist "New World Order" that conspiracy theorists cringe at, and a Nazi like William Dudley Pelley must have dreamed of.

Williamson himself later left Noblesville to join Adamski, and to contact (via "automatic writing") a bewildering list of Space Brothers and "Ascended Masters" including (but we're sure not limited to): *Actar* of Mercury, *Adu* of Hatonn in Andromeda, *Agfa Affa* from Uranus, *Ankar-22* of Jupiter, *Artok* of Pluto, *Awa* from Outer Space, *Garr* from Pluto, *Kadar Lacu* from Saturn, *Karas* the Space Brother, *Lomec* of Venus, *Nah-9* from Neptune, *Noro* of the Saucer Fleet, *Oara* of Saturn, *Ponnar* of *Hatoon*, *Regga* of Mars, *Ro* of *Torresoton*, *Sedat* of *Hatonn*, *Suttku* of Saturn, *Terra* of Venus, *Wan-4* of the *Safanian* planets, *Zago* of Mars and *Zo* of Neptune.

(Whew! That's quite an exhaustive social register.)

Pelley's organization still exists, although it has apparently relocated itself from Indiana to Oregon. A quick perusal of its website reveals it to be much in line with similar organizations, with on-line texts of many messages received "clairaudient" through the mediumistic abilities of William Dudley Pelley.

Mr. Pelley died in Noblesville in 1965.

A far-less controversial and far more mysterious Indiana native was Terre Haute's own Richard Zenor, the psychic medium who founded the "Agasha Temple of Wisdom."

Information on the life of Mr. Zenor is scarce, but a sort of thumbnail biography is available in journalist James Crenshaw's book, *Telephone Between Worlds*.

It was this book, humble reader, that the present author happened upon one fine day, when, suddenly, something (some still small voice inside) told him to leave his apartment, and go upstairs, to the laundry room, where something special would be waiting for him. This has often happened to me before, in the case of special "gifts" from Spirit, and it is always a pleasure to happen upon some rare item that suddenly, mysteriously, happens to fall into our mystified fingertips.

Such was the case with the book *Telephone Between Worlds*

Apparently, young Richard began early in his mediumship. He was strange, quiet child, often given to talking to "invisible friends." Since children are often known to strike up acquaintances purely from their own imaginations, Richard's mother must have surely dismissed this out of hand, at least for a time.

In school, Richard often knew the answer to the most serious, pressing questions before everyone else did, a fact that could not have much endeared him to his fellow classmates. However, Richard, as strange and quiet and "gifted" as he appeared to be, was apparently just getting started.

He began to go into "trances," and would commence to stay in a vague, coma-like condition, necessitating a complete removal from the school premises. His mother, who must have been at her wits end, decided finally to seek out "spiritual advice" in the form of taking the boy to a mediumistic circle.

It was during this séance that Richard's talents began to suddenly burst forth. He demonstrated his ability at "trumpet" (or bringing forth spirit voices with the aid of an aluminum trumpet) and also of "materialization" (the act of bringing spirits into the room in material form), levitation, and bringing forth "apports" (the act of materializing objects from a distance, often lost objects teleported from a great distance, or objects that have never been known to exist in the first place).

Furthermore, his mother could have been no less disturbed to find that her son, at times, would mysteriously begin to float or levitate upwards himself.

Curiously fantastic episodes can be recounted in the strange life of Richard Zenor. His own sister once said that he caused a "life-like" apparition of a dear friend to appear before her, even though that friend had passed on some months beforehand. And then, of course, there was the incident involving one of Richard's visions actually saving his own father's life.

His father, who owned an interest in a Colorado coal mine, was disturbed by the recurring vision the boy had of seeing an explosion at a mine, and many men being killed as a result. His wife was so distressed that she begged him to stay away from the place (he had been planning to go there on a business excursion), and he, perhaps grudgingly, obliged her. Sure enough, it was on the appointed day when he would have been touring the facility that an accident with dynamite occurred, and many men *were* killed. Many, that is, except for Richard Zenor's father, who had been warned in advance.

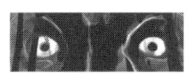

As if all of this weren't startling enough, Richard was also given to taking "astral fights" and once recounted that, as he lay upstairs in his room napping, his "astral body" issued forth from his physical one, and took a brief excursion, following his father around on his daily business.

When the old man finally got home, tired after a long day of work, he grumpily set about informing his housewife of all that he had had to accomplish in such a short time. She cut him off abruptly, however, informing him that Richard had already filled her in all of the man's daily activities, so there was no need to go through it all again. Richard's father must have been, duly, unnerved.

(We may be so bold as state here that it is darn lucky for him he seems to have been a fellow that rarely strayed from the "straight and narrow.")

Richard was soon known as the "Wonder Boy" around town, and his escapades even include helping to find buried treasure in Colorado. More important than this, however, was the new phase that Richard's strange gifts began to enter as he quickly realized he no longer needed the aluminum trumpet as a means to call forth "voices," but instead could produce a multiplicity of spirit voices and strange personalities simply by lapsing into the now familiar trance state. His new method of mediumship was soon attracting not dozens, or even hundreds, but thousands of people to come and hear him pronounce (or rather, hear the spirits pronounce) on a startling range of topics.

A number of eminent psychologists and doctors were consulted, and examined the boy, pronouncing him completely normal. They, themselves, must have been scratching their heads, for the great many personalities and obscure facts and information that poured forth from Richard were, surely, beyond the meager abilities of a young child to either intentionally or unintentionally fake.

Indeed, an eminent doctor followed Richard on a cross-country tour, and wrote him a glowing appraisal on December 18th, 1930, stating:

> *"My Dear Richard:*
>
> *"As our trip is about to close and we will, for awhile, at least, separate, I want to express to you some of the thoughts and convictions I have experienced, while with you.*
>
> *"Although feeling that a future life was essential to make the life on earth reasonable and just, I have not for many years been able to believe in a future existence. Most doctors share with me this conviction. But after being with you, and witnessing the demonstrations through your mediumship, I have no other alternative than to be convinced, intellectually, that we go on living after we pass through Death…*
>
> *"…This appreciation is shared with the vast majority of those with whom we have come in contact, and I know that in every town you have left behind many sincere friends and converts to Spiritualism…"*

And Richard Zenor had hundreds of such letters in his collection.

It was during a demonstration at a church in Los Angeles that journalist James Crenshaw first met Richard Zenor, and found himself impressed by the mediumistic demonstration. He also relates an amusing tale concerning a less-than-scrupulous photographer who attempted to cheat Richard out of his hard-earned money by selling him some (obviously) fraudulent "spirit photographs." (Popular during the heyday of Spiritualism, such photographs were usually made by appointment, wherein the unsuspecting "mark" would pay an exorbitant fee to a charlatan "spirit photographer" to sit for a photograph in which a dead relative or loved one was said to appear. These were almost always crude fakes.)

Crenshaw would go on to make an entire study of Richard Zenor, summarizing his life's work and teachings in the book *Telephone Between Worlds*. Although he started out as a hard-nosed journalist, a true skeptic, he later became convinced that Richard Zenor was the genuine article: a man who could communicate with the "Master Teachers," as well as the spirits of the departed.

One such spirit was the departed husband of a woman named Thelma Turner, who was so impressed with Richard she went on, eventually, to become Mrs. Richard Zenor. Zenor was apparently able to contact her husband, confirmed by several important details that would have been known only to him, such as her purchase of a string of costume pearls, and the outcome of a legal action taken by her mother.

Richard, who left his physical body behind, allowing it to be occupied by other spirits (and safeguarded by "Dr. Navajo," his "Red Indian" control), was able to speak, when in this trance state, in a variety of different voices, and even other languages, as well as mimic the physical mannerisms of people that had, supposedly died (and who, during their lifetimes, were completely unknown to him). The value and quality of his information—which came from not only those spirits who had "passed on," but from "Master Teachers" (such as Agasha), who had reached an elevated spiritual state of vibration, and who were prepared to hold forth on any number of philosophical points, as well as pontificate about the meaning of life, death, and the future—was nearly undisputed.

Author Crenshaw relates to us an astonishing story of "Margery," one of Richard Zenor's regular "controls," and how, during one session of channeling, this control slipped away to Crenshaw's house, where his wife was alone, busily typing out a letter and making coffee, as well as setting out breakfast dishes. When the spirit returned to speak through Richard, she related to Crenshaw what had been occurring in his home while he was away, which he was, only hours later, able to confirm with his wife, perfectly.

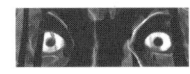

It was from Richard Zenor's most committed sitters that he drew together his circle of students, a group that would later be formed into the Agasha Temple of Wisdom (www.agasha.org). According to their website, they teach their disciples that:

> I SHALL STRIVE TO LEARN TO BE THAT WHICH I AM.
>
> I WILL ENDEAVOR TO UNDERSTAND ALL EXPERIENCES I HAVE YET TO EXPERIENCE.
>
> I AM THAT I AM SO ALL MAY BE.
>
> I SHALL LEARN THAT THERE IS NO PEACE THAT LIES IN TOMORROW THAT IS NOT HERE TODAY.
>
> I WILL BE THE PURE COLOR OF ALL MY COLLECTIVE EXPERIENCE AND I SHALL CALL THAT MY LIGHT, AND THAT LIGHT OF PUREST WHITE SHALL SHINE AS A BEACON FOR ALL TO SEE.

Furthermore, we find on their website that Agasha was one of many great teachers 7,000 years ago who met in Egypt to study "Universal God Consciousness," and that these Master Teachers devised "inter-transitory" mediumship to convey this ancient wisdom teachings to a world that would, thousands of years later, be needing it. This involved changing the very metabolism of the (unborn?) medium in a way that seems highly confusing. And who, you may ask, was the first "inter-transitory" medium? Yep, you guessed it: Richard Zenor.

The group itself seems to be obscure, and has obviously expanded on the teachings of Richard Zenor in the past decades, although they do offer the book *Telephone Between Worlds* for sale on their website, and encourage the reading of it as one of their principal texts,

As for the book itself, we thought we would leave you with a small portion of the "Teachings of Agasha," as they are reproduced in the back of the book.

> *"Many of you will not reach the period after 1965 when peace will be established on earth, but you will be able to assist and observe from the spiritual realms. You are now going through one of the most trying periods the world has ever known, and millions will have their trials and tribulations. Live your life fully and normally from day to day and know that God—the Christ-self within you—will protect you according to the light of your understanding."*

Richard Zenor departed our dimension in 1978.

18

Slithery Somethings

The subject of lake monsters will, invariably, bring up a smile to the face of most individuals, who remember a particularly poorly-faked photograph allegedly of the "Loch Ness Monster" that has been reprinted *ad nauseum* for several decades now. The photo, showing a curling, snake-like head peeping above the water, is quite obviously that of a simple floating toy. Nothing remarkable about it.

However, in much the same way that Hairy Whatsits have been reported in regions as far removed from each other as the Himalayas and the American Pacific Northwest, so to do Slithery Somethings seem to range far and wide across the face of the globe. We have them in Indiana as surely as they have them in Scotland, and ours seem to be no less frightening or real to those that witness them.

The idea of underwater monsters brings to mind the many-tentacled terrors depicted in the stories of horror (some would claim "occult") author H.P. Lovecraft. Although we can't boast a monster nearly half as grotesque as the watery Cthulu (who, according to Lovecraft's famous stories, lies in sunken *R'lyah*, dreaming), we can boast the hideous "Manitou," which comes from the Native American term for having a connection to the Great Spirit.

The Manitou (also variously reported to have been called "Meshakenabek") were a trio of monsters that dwelt beneath Lake Manitou in Rochester, each a tentacled beast hungry for the flesh of the deer and other small animals that came to the water's edge to drink. Finally, after the monster emerged from the deep of the "black river" to wreak havoc on the nearby Indian village one terrible day, powerful magic is said to have been used to dispel the Manitou from their place in the lake, and all was well (although we wonder if the Manitou was ever known to thrust their tentacles out of the water to grasp at humans, hence the need for the exorcism).

Perhaps, though, the magic spell either wore off, or was not completely successful, for in 1827, the beast was apparently spotted by workmen endeavoring to build a grain mill for the Pottawatomie. The creature was described by a nervous witness as: "The head being

about three feet across the frontal bone and having something of the contour of a beef's head, but the neck tapering and having the character of a serpent; color dingy with large yellow spots."

Nasty looking beast, we must assume. Down through the years, the Manitou (or, perhaps, there was really more than one?) was known to rear its head above the waters of Lake Manitou from time to time, and thoroughly frighten and mystify any witnesses. Alternately described as a "monstrous squid" or a "monstrous, oversized fish," it was most generally agreed that it was an unknown.

For a time, the mystery seemed to have been solved, when a gigantic buffalo carp was reeled in as the probable culprit in the Manitou sightings. However, this explanation soon failed to account for all possible sightings, as did likewise a one hundred and sixteen pound spoon fish that was displayed for a time as the "Manitou."

At any rate, there hasn't been a sighting of the "Manitou Monster" in over a century, although locals might tell you differently.

A much more interesting legendry lake beast is "Oscar," usually dubbed the "beast of Busco," an immensely old critter that is said to have been seen near Blue Lake in Churubusco, Indiana.

Accounts seem to vary widely concerning, exactly what Oscar is, or even what he looks like. Some have him a wild, hairy creature (not unlike a Bigfoot) known to prey on small animals, and disappear into the lake when not so occupied. Others tell of a "sea serpent" in the traditional sense, a sort of Indiana "Nessie" known to bob and undulate into view just above the icy surface of the lake for curious and astounded onlookers, from time to time. Still others claim that

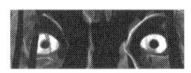

Oscar is an enormous mutant turtle (seemingly deathless).

Whatever the case, one story has a duo of fisherman spotting their "Oscar" (which made an appearance in the guise of a monstrous sea serpent, this time), and, duly terrified, rowing for shore in a tizzy of panicked fright. They then, resolutely, set up several search parties, whose chief find was a series of bizarre tracks. But no Oscar, unfortunately.

Another story places the blame on Oscar for the mutilated and missing livestock of a local farmer, who first began to lose chickens, and then finally entire cows, to something that was sneaking off with his animals in the middle of the night. Whatever Oscar might be then, we can assume he had (or has?) a big appetite…

Reportedly, the farmer caught sight of Oscar one day, basking on the edge of the lake, and realized that he was a fifteen-foot snapping turtle. Horrified at this colossal freak, he quickly assembled help in an attempt to chain and capture the creature. His plans soon fell asunder however, when the stout horses being used to pull the length of chains (which some brave soul had apparently managed to bind the monster turtle with) found themselves unable to pull the mutant to captivity, and the chains themselves were snapped. Oscar disappeared beneath the rippling, cool surface of the lake, falling into the murk, but living forever in local folklore.

According to Wikipedia (an online source for which the veracity of all their claims and information we can not, presently, vouch safe) there are no fewer than six lakes in Indiana sporting some variation of a "monster" or "serpent" of unknown origin. Other sources put the number at twice that, or a little over. Suffice it to say, if you are ever out fishing, and you feel a tug at the line, an almighty big tug, just stop and consider how much work you want to put in reeling in whatever is biting the end of your line.

You might pull up something stranger than the daily catch.

19

The Phantom Soldiers of Tippecanoe

Some memories, some tragedies, never die, and some curses seem to live on forever in the bones and sinews of the people who occupy a land and a history, collectively. Further, some individuals, in a kind of dualistic, metaphysical framework, seem to alternate pathways in history that forever link them, strangely, in a sort of historical diptych.

Such might be the case with Tippecanoe, and Tecumseh.

William Henry Harrison, the scion of wealthy parents from Richmond, Virginia, was drawn, by a perplexing sense of rebellion, perhaps, to a hard and dangerous life in the military service of the fledgling nation, and fought valiantly in the Indian wars along the territory that one day become Ohio and Indiana, quickly rising to the rank of Lieutenant. He was finally appointed governor of Indiana Territory by none other than President John Adams, and served in the capacities of congressman, senator, Ambassador to Columbia, and finally, was elected President of the United States, a position that did not bode well for him, considering he contracted a fatal bought of pneumonia on his Inauguration Day. Thirty-one days later he was dead, and his successor, President Tyler, finished out his ill-fated term.

Of course, the popular political slogan from 1840 'Tippecanoe and Tyler, too," arose both from the fact that John Tyler was Harrison's running-mate, and that Harrison himself was well-renowned for his victorious battle against the Shawnee, on the Tippecanoe River, northeast of present-day Lafayette.

It was as governor that Harrison (who, not altogether a bad fellow, made illegal the sale of liquor to Indians, as well as ensured that they were all inoculated against smallpox) had arranged for a land grab of three million acres of Indian territory on the Wabash and White rivers, an act that enraged Tecumseh, the fiery leader of the Shawnee, as well as his brother, Tenskwatawa, also know as "The Prophet."

113

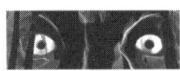

In a desperate measure to incite insurgent forces, the ailing Chief of the Shawnee and his mysterious brother began a journey southward, trying desperately to enlist the aid of friendly tribes of Sioux, Apache, and Alabama in a full-on assault to drive the White settlers "into the sea."

Although he was successful in some respects, the aged leader met with scorn in many territories, including derision from a scoffing tribe of Alabama that made their home on the banks of the Mississippi. They told him, essentially, that "talk was cheap."

Enraged at the insolence of the Alabama warriors, Tecumseh pronounced a righteous curse, telling them that he would one day stamp his foot on the ground "and make their wigwams fall down."

It was only a short time later, December 16, 1811, that the most violent earthquake in U.S. history erupted. The New Madrid Earthquake, with casualties ranging in the thousands, shook much of the Middle West, sent the Mighty Mississippi roiling in a reverse direction (not doing much for the fabled riverboats who set course upon her waters) and churned up an estimated forty thousand square miles. Of course, the Alabama found themselves chastised, terrified, and perhaps duly impressed.

At any rate, their wigwams did, indeed, fall to the ground.

Tecumseh had succeeded in raising his army of insurgents, and they began a terror campaign against settlers along the Wabash River Valley. Sensing that the situation was growing bloody and desperate, Governor Harrison established a fort at Terre Haute. He had taken control of the Indiana Territory Militia, and later that would prove to be for the best.

In short order, they would begin ethnic cleansing operations to remove the last of the Native Americans from Federal land. They would be largely successful at this.

The Prophet, not content to sit back while his people were dispossessed, fomented a special plan of attack. As militia troops approached the mouth of the Tippecanoe River, The Prophet sent out a special delegate to appeal for a meeting between The Prophet and Harrison. The officers agreed to this plea, but were duly suspicious. They had every right to be.

It was a cold, wet morning, November 7th, 1811, when scores of Shawnee descended upon the Indiana Militia fighters, who had thoughtfully slept in their uniforms with weapons ready at their sides. They woke up, quickly, to a bloody and fatal melee, but one which they could not have doubted would eventually ensue.

The resulting fight saw casualties mount on both sides, with over sixty militiamen killed and a hundred wounded, and scores of

Shawnee lying dead. The wails of agony and the sense of terror and pain must have been very real and thick in the air that whole, long day, so it is little wonder that such impressions may have become "imprinted," in a sense, in the surrounding environment. More on that in a moment.

The Prophet and his surviving men beat a hasty retreat, and Harrison now took a more "pro-active" (some would say "bloodthirsty") approach to cleansing federal lands of Native Americans. As for Tecumseh, who had been away at the time of the assault, he was most displeased with The Prophet for bungling what he felt would have been a far more successful plan to drive out the White settlers.

(What that plan might have entailed, we are unaware, yet, if Tecumseh is to be judged based on his skill at "making the earth tremble," we feel it must have been a whopper.)

The both of them Tecumseh and Tenskwatawa both eventually fled to Canada, where they aided the British in the War of 1812. It was apparently another losing proposition for the duo, as Tecumseh met his end at the Battle of Thames, near Ontario. The Indian wars in the Middle west were essentially over, with his passing, and it soon became apparent, even to the British, that the Americans were here to stay.

Harrison, of course, met his end thirty-two days into his Presidency, and what should have been the very pinnacle of his career turned into dismal tragedy for him. Tecumseh's curse come 'round, perhaps? Like every tragic event involving a great or respected figure, tongues will wag and gossip and folklore will take hold, after a period of time.

What is beyond dispute is the seeming residual psychic energies, and bizarre haunting forces, that swirl around the route that General Harrison's troops took to get to their fatal, famous battle. An old two-story house that looks out on that route is said (we presume by those who have resided there) to echo, on chill November nights, with the stamping of many marching boots, and the ghostly roll of an old drum. The land, apparently, acts as an "auditory channel" to a past that is still occurring: when brave militiamen and desperate Natives were heading on a collision course toward history in a battle that might still be occurring, somewhere, in some sector of the space-time continuum—in spirit, if not in flesh and bone.

Thus, we have the Phantom Soldiers of Tippecanoe. Onward they march, perhaps forever…

20

The Chain

Can an evil act, like a morbid stain, be passed down through the echoing ages in the form of an odd mark on a physical object? That's the subject of this delightful little drama that could be most adequately entitled: The Chain.

Once, in the cozy town of Orleans, a young woman became betrothed to a man many years her senior. He had, during the brief, fiery courtship, seemed to be everything that a naïve young woman could hope for. He was courteous, kind, forgiving, tolerant, generous, handsome, and, best of all, he was rich. The young woman felt that she had had her future handed to her by her better angels, and agreed in short order to become the man's young bride.

The honeymoon was not to last very long, however. While the young woman obediently and tolerantly began to assume what, for the time, were common wifely duties, the man went about the important business of making money and securing their place as prominent, wealthy leaders of their little Indiana community. While the woman might have felt a little stifled, at times, by the increasingly strident demands and seeming perfectionism of her new husband, these were not so intolerable at first, and she bore them accordingly. However, she was soon to discover the meaning behind the old phrase "buyer's remorse."

A swift downturn in the local economy, and some unwise business transactions, soon left the husband heavily in debt, and his business teetered on the edge of collapse. The husband grew from being occasionally irritable and sometimes brooding, to downright petty, cruel…and even violent. The wife stoically bore the brunt of her husband's wrath to the limits of her endurance, praying that his business would improve after this rough patch, and that all could then be well again.

Alas, it was not to be, and, as feverishly as he worked to right whatever it was that had gone wrong, he soon found himself in the position of selling his house and his property, and moving his wife and he to a smaller, far less luxuriant home in the country. His wife submitted to this new change of affairs with little complaint, but with a growing sense of dissatisfaction as to the course her fate had taken.

The husband, now feverishly working day and night to try and recoup the vast wealth that had seemingly slipped through his fingers, paid little attention to his new bride...or anything else for that matter.

He spent untold hours alone in the darkness of his study, going over and over deeds and papers, and the only company he allowed was the occasional barrister or business partner. His wife, now forced to tiptoe around him lest he be disturbed and fly into one of his famous rages, was content to merely bring him his meals, and sneak away as quietly as she could, hiding herself in her room after her housework was completed and often crying herself to sleep.

Her husband often simply slept in his chair. He had grown haggard, and his hair, once lustrous and black, had grown thin and started to fall out in clumps. Furthermore, he had taken to drinking at all hours of the day and night, venturing out of his room, at times, with a half-bottle of spirits in his hand and a mean, discontented leer on his face.

He would storm and rage at his "enemies," talk to people who weren't there, and generally made himself as much of a terror as can possibly be imagined. Meanwhile, their financial situation grew more and more precarious.

In the midst of all this unhappiness, the wife, who was by now completely neglected by her increasing erratic and bizarre husband, soon began to develop a plan to make her escape. She planned on leaving in the dead of night, when her husband would long since be passed out from strong drink, and to do this she enlisted the help of a local field hand, who could be counted on to bring round a horse and carriage and see her off to safety. Then, she would take a train back to her family, and file for divorce.

She anxiously packed a few things, careful to hide this away in her closet under a bundle of blankets lest her husband accidentally discover what she was planning.

Finally, the appointed day of her escape loomed, and she went downstairs to listen to the harsh snoring of her spouse as he reclined, drunkenly, in front of his desk. She went back upstairs, fetched her bag, and then crept down. Already, she could hear the tramp of hooves coming up the road.

She hurried across the foyer, when suddenly, tragically, a voice called out, "Where do you think you're going?"

Her husband, for once, had not been drunk at all. May even, in fact, have somehow guessed her intentions, as now he stepped from the shadows with a look of sheer, exultant fury covering his haggard face.

In his hand he held a length of ugly, rusted chain.

Before she could answer, or even gain another foot in front of him, he began to swing the chain down upon her pretty face, his yells and imprecations echoing loudly through the empty house as barren, loveless walls gave mute testimony to murder. Outside, the hooves continued to beat their staccato rhythm upon the road, but the driver would never deliver

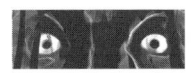

his secret passenger to her destination. By the time he came to the door of the mansion, the woman was dead. The husband had, apparently, fled the scene in disgust with what he had just done.

Of course, it was only a short time before the foul deed the man had committed was avenged. A short trial followed, but the evidence of his guilt was never really in question and the man was sentenced to hang. His sentence carried out, his body was interred in the local cemetery, beneath a rather nice headstone. It was then that the bizarre echo of past misdeeds began to take shape in the form of a strange stain that worked its way, inch by inch, across the rough surface at the side of the headstone. This stone, amazingly enough, seemed to bear the form of a chain, and it was not long before it was being whispered that the image itself was a message from beyond the grave, living testament to the crime committed by the old man, as well as a sort of curse to anyone who would dare come out to the cemetery on a full moon night, and utter the old man's name (which, incidentally, was PRUETT).

The story does not end there, however. It is told often that two men, psychic investigators from Washington, D.C., who found out about the mysterious chain by happenstance, made the trip to the tiny Indiana town to investigate the matter for themselves.

The arrived at the cemetery well before sundown, and commenced to seek out the old headstone. After finding it easily enough, one of the men pronounced himself unimpressed, and decided that he would wait back at the car. The other took a sample of the crumbling old thing for analysis, and snapped a few photographs, before rejoining his companion.

They started off for their hotel, each a little disappointed that the infamous gravestone had proved so unremarkable and mundane (one of them felt that the image of the chain had most likely been inscribed on the surface of the marble by accident when the stone was being hoisted into place), when, suddenly, behind them began to glow a strange brilliance.

The men, at first, assumed it to be nothing more than the reflection of the headlights off a cemetery monument, but the driver sped up a little, nervously.

They found themselves amazed to realize that the light, indeed, seemed to be following the car!

Panicking, the driver turned a corner too quickly, and the car sped off the road into a line of old fence posts, actually turning over as it flew to a crashing halt.

The passenger was thrown from the car, but managed, miraculously, to pick himself up and walk away unscathed. The driver, however, was not so fortunate.

His throat had been cut, and his mangled body had become wrapped, bizarrely, in a rusted length of chain.

Believe it if you will.

Insert image 22 with the following text

21

Sister Sarah

The legend of Sister Sarah is long, tangled, and confusing. The problem being, chiefly, that no one can agree, exactly, just who Sister Sarah was. Some have her as a murderous nun, a woman who slew infants in her charge and later, when hanged for her crime, proved remorseless before God and man. Others tell a darker tale of an old witch, a local crone said to consort with the Devil, and cast curses, as well as divine accidents and bad tidings for the future of the community. These legends are long, and in Fulton County, when you say the name "Sister Sarah" you open up a can of local folklore and speculation brimming with colorful (some might say colorless… as in grim) anecdotes.

Sister Sarah is also said to have been a young woman who became pregnant, perhaps through an act of incestuous rape, who then flung herself, to her death out of the top window of her own home. What can be said for certain is that the grave Sister Sarah is buried in, is in the family plot of the Daniel P. McIntire Cemetery. And local teenagers, each eager to scare each other, and themselves, to silliness, have woven an entire macabre web of legendry around what one must do (and what may, verily, befall the misfortunate) should they endeavor to raise Sister Sarah from her long, decrepit slumber.

One legend has it that if you leave an empty glass at the grave of Sister Sarah, when you return in the morning, the glass will be full of blood. Perhaps that's a bit sensational for most people to swallow, so here's another tidbit.

Apparently, if you stand at her grave, and call her name out three times in unison, the apparition herself will appear, slowly, in a cloud of smoke. What on earth could happen next can only be a matter of conjecture, but if this particular means of summoning has ever been successfully attempted, we have no record of it.

The ghost herself (itself), is said to wander, as many a ghost often does, through the misty grounds of the cemetery at nightfall, holding a candle in one hand, and with an utter look of mournful intensity over a life lived, and lost (we must assume by all the variant accounts) badly.

Whatever the objective reality concerning Sister Sarah, and her ghostly habits, one thing can be ascertained for certain: the house abutting the sacred grounds of the Daniel P. McIntire cemetery has its fair share of odd phenomenon and residually woeful feelings. Just ask "Robert," who once resided in the house, and can attest to the fact that there is quite a bit of haunting energy lurking about the grounds.

According to Robert, the house he and his family resided in was most definitely haunted by the presence of a female, one dubbed "Sarah" by the family, who never really considered her a nuisance, but who did have a handful of frightening encounters with her. Of course, there were the typical "cold spots," and the creeping feelings of "being watched" and of not quite being alone, when one was alone.

A much more frightening occurrence is one we have already visited several times in the course of this book, and shall be visiting again, and that is the phenomenon of "bedroom apparitions." A not-altogether unusual occurrence, this typically involves someone waking up from slumber and seeing a ghost. Or an "Old Hag." Or even a "little gray man" from Zeta Reticuli (or possibly another dimension in the fabric of the space/time continuum) ready to whisk them away to a hovering UFO. Sometimes (as we will find later in the course of this book), the apparition is a vilely malevolent "hooded man," a character in a black cloak with a hood and no face. This character is said to be immensely large, have long, skinny black fingers (like blackened bones), no face, and a pair of burning eyes.

In other words, it's a demonic picture of the classical Grim Reaper come to life.

The reality of such apparitions, however, is debatable. Whereas occultists might give utterance to "spirits" or even "demons" as their possible genus of origin, the more level-headed and scientific will put it down to "sleep paralysis," and resultant hallucinations. Sleep paralysis, a physiological condition in which the sleeper awakes, paralyzed with fear, and certain that a malevolent presence is in the room with them, is often accompanied by vivid hallucinations; culled, we suppose, from the night-tide of dreaming brains jarred, for unexplained reasons, into a half-wakefulness.

Other (usually) self-appointed experts will say that the "sleep paralysis" explanation is, itself, rather farfetched, considering some of the experiences reported by those troubled with these remarkably terrifying nighttime disturbances.

Of course, we've traveled somewhat far from the grounds of the Daniel P. McIntire cemetery and the house on the grounds occupied by Robert and his family. One night, while they were both sleeping fitfully, feeling a mysterious chill, possibly, waft through the room, a mysterious event transpired. Perhaps Robert rolled over, eager to get up and close the window against the cold.

At any rate, he got more than he bargained for upon awakening, for, as he lay there in bed, he suddenly realized that he and his wife, indeed, were not alone in the room.

According to Robert, far from being paralyzed with fear (which if the case, would of course suggest that he was simply experiencing "sleep paralysis"), he claims to have awakened his wife, who came to wakefulness, and saw the same disturbing vision as himself.

A ghostly woman in a white robe, holding a candle, with a strange, mournful countenance about her, was floating at the edge of their bed. Floated, in fact, around the room, before disappearing through the closed door. She had long, flowing hair, he recalled.

Also, she was missing a face.

That, alone, would be enough to send most people running for the rafters.

However, Robert and his family, apparently, were made of sterner stuff.

Trying as best they could to put the unsettling incident out of their minds, the family apparently went about their lives with little interruption from the subtle presence of the supernatural Sarah. That is, until one night, when Robert, downstairs and up late, heard the scamper of what sounded to be little feet on the landing upstairs.

Annoyed that his daughters should be up past their bedtimes, he went upstairs with a huff, in the darkness, to root out any mischief of which his offspring might be clandestinely engaged.

Yet, climbing the stairs in the dark, he was not greeted with the scampering forms of one of his children, but something far more disturbing. (Some would say wondrous. Others would envy him.)

There stood Sarah, in all of her ghostly glory: same flowing, light-colored robe, same long, flowing hair. He never said whether or not she was wearing what approximated a human face at this particular juncture, but we can assume, happily I think, she must not have forgotten it this time.

Then, just as quickly, she faded from view, leaving Robert a puzzled, frightened, curious, unhappy, but altogether intrigued man. (We haven't personally interviewed him, so this particular mélange of emotions is entirely based upon a solipsistic ideation of how we, ourselves, might feel if confronted by such a sudden, striking phenomenon. And we have been so confronted, in the past.)

The only tumult Sister Sarah ever engendered was the veritable destruction of that most commonplace of all American family holiday ornamentations: the Christmas tree.

One Christmas, perhaps it was even Christmas Day, Sarah decided she most certainly didn't like the Christmas tree that was blocking

the way of her invisible perambulations, and suddenly, and most abruptly and without the slightest measure of consideration (even for a ghost) she proceeded to overturn the thing, scattering ornaments and pine needles everywhere. It was a real four-alarm mess, and Robert was certain it was either the fault of the resident ghost, or the family pooch.

The dog, though, had spent a shivery December evening outdoors, certainly bewailing his sorry lot, and wondering why he couldn't have been so blessed as to have a family that cared to have him indoors for the evening. Hence, the blame fell, quite naturally, on Sister Sarah, who played

only a few additional small pranks, such as overturning pictures and moving objects about. All common enough folderol for resident spooks.

If any of Our Readers are curious as to the actual identity of this somewhat talked-about little lady, whose very moniker conjures up images of mystery and fear, well, all we can say is, good luck to you in ascertaining which Sister Sarah is which.

There are no less than *three* Sarah McIntire's in the family history, but we're betting it is the "Sarah" (maiden name "Hoover") who went mad and jumped to her death out of an upper story window of the old place on November 4th, 1873. Seems likely enough.

Imagine, driven mad in one brief moment (or was it a lingering brain disease? We may never know), and suddenly deciding that life on this Earth was so far from being livable that one would be willing to jump, through a pane of solid glass, to a hard, bitter, painful death below.

Or maybe she had some help on the way down. Who can now say with any certainty?

At any rate, her last moments were either spent bleeding, cut in a million places, with every significant bone broken in her body, and staring out at the grounds of her once happy home as she, quite literally, "gave up the ghost." Or, they were spent in a bed, at a hospital (but more likely in her own bed) where she, quite shortly, succumbed to her massive injuries.

At any rate, if you visit the Daniel P. McIntire cemetery any time soon, be sure to draw up a glass of water to bring with you. Pour it out over the grave of Sister Sarah, and leave it for the night. Drive back down Fort Wayne Road the next day, and retrieve it. If it *is* filled with blood in the morning, drop us a line. Please.

We sure are curious to know.

22

Culbertson Mansion

There are dark places in the world where evil, pain, and suffering seem to accrue, over the years, building force like some sort of macabre battery of psychic malevolence. Such places play out their little scenes, rehearsing endlessly their strange, surreal scenarios again and again, throughout history. One such place is the Tower of London, the fabled English prison where men have met death and torture down through the centuries. It is said that the ghost of Ann Boleyn can be heard running, screaming through the passageways of the old place; running, we must assume, from the executioners.

Other reports have her showing up, sans head. Ann lost hers on the chopping block at the orders of an irate Henry the Eighth, whose historical record might suggest he was, perhaps a tad unbalanced, when it came to affairs of the heart.

Some even suggest Ann still walks the grounds of the Tower, *holding* her severed head. We're sure that must be some sight for the casual tourist.

A little closer to home, in New Albany, such a repository of the "dead, stifling" energy of a not-quite-quieted past is the Culbertson Mansion, a stately old place that is now on the registry of State Historic Sites.

Built in 1867 by millionaire William S. Culbertson, the place cost him a hefty (in those days) $120,000, and encompassed twenty-five opulent rooms, a true American castle in the middle of what was, at the time, the largest city in Indiana.

The years have not worn the building down much either. It is still the great, brooding edifice it once was so many long decades ago, still holding within itself the secrets and sins, the shuddering legends and lore that encompass its history and augment its unique grandeur. Truly, if walls could talk…

Those particular walls, we think, might tell a tale both regal and repellent, for it was here that lavish parties were hosted, fine wine was toasted, gala dances and gourmet dinners were eaten, and children were, quite possibly, abused. At the least, emotionally. For it was well-known that the Culbertson family was strict with discipline (one wonders what tales the servants told when they finally resigned their positions).

William Culbertson amassed a fortune in his lifetime, having a hand in dry goods, the Kentucky-Indiana Railroad, and starting up a utility service. Fortune had smiled upon him in life, and he had even netted a comely wife, Cornelia. (Could you imagine a more suitable name for the tale we are about to relate?)

The place was designed to the finest specifications, and the portraits of both William and Cornelia Culbertson, restored to their former glory and watching over the residence from the prison of their wooden frames, greet any visitor to Culbertson mansion who may happen to stroll in, to witness a part of Indiana history that has been laboriously preserved.

Perhaps, though, William and Cornelia are still watching over the stately old home in other ways, too.

Those who have worked at the home report that they have experienced a feeling of having a "presence" with them, particularly when working on the third floor. Of course, one supposes such a presence could be felt all over the house at various "high times" of activity, but ghosts often do seem to have special rooms or areas they frequent, even in some small homes.

(Why this is, is a matter of conjecture. Perhaps the spirit liked or felt compelled to a certain area of the home, or still feels territorial about this area for some reason. Perhaps ghosts don't "really" know they're dead, and some of them get caught in a sort of metaphysical "feedback loop" where they feel compelled to perform the same actions, over and over, ad infinitum, for decades and even centuries. Perhaps they are simply "energy forms" that leave imprints, like a video recording, in the environment around them, and that these "imprints" or recordings can be picked-up on by sensitive souls when they come into the particular area. Perhaps all of these, or some combination, or none of them, could account for it.

A far stranger theory is that *All of Reality As We Know It* is nothing more than a giant recording, like a metaphysical DVD, and that our consciousness is the laser playing the particular spot on the DVD we think of as "present day" reality. Everything has already happened, the End and the Beginning are One, and History is going on simultaneously in different dimensions. Ghosts then, are simply reflections from that other dimension, when the laser beam of consciousness "skips" or plays the incorrect groove, or two grooves nearly simultaneously. It is much like a regular DVD player that sometimes freezes up or does funny things, superimposing one scene over another, or meshing the whole thing together in a rather frightening matrix of pixilated images that deform different scenes into each other. So it is, some theorize, that our "Holographic Universe" is apt to let a lusty belch, misdirect consciousness, and have the whole thing helter skelter. Then Victorian women suddenly end up popping about, doing their daily chores, at odd intervals, in the world of 2008. In some sense, they are simply reflections of what is going on "over there," in that area of the Great DVD that our consciousness is not focusing on. Of course, those who ascribe to this theory usually believe we are all simply ONE consciousness anyway, schizophrenically fragmented into a myriad of "broken glass" consciousnesses—to go any further with any of this highfalutin speculation would threaten to make this the longest digression in ghostly literary history.

It is on the historic third floor, a place that was sealed off after the Culbertson's sold the house in 1899, that the ghostly presence can be most easily felt and ascertained. Those who work at the historic site have complained of prankish ghosts that like to start and stop vacuum cleaners, as well as spread dried floral arrangements over newly-vacuumed rugs. Some workers find themselves perplexed by this; still others shrug it off as part of the price to be paid for working long hours in a stately old residence.

Although the third floor of Culbertson Mansion has been used, at various times by groups such as the American Legion (who retained it, oddly enough, as a converted pool hall for a little while), it was never completely restored, and when the Department of Parks and Natural Resources acquired it in the mid-seventies, the third floor was in a deplorable condition, rife with the skeletons of old birds, pile of their old droppings, and whatever refuse anyone who had ever owned the edifice ever decided to dump there. It took months for workers to clean it out, but one worker in particular caught a glimpse of something extraordinary as she went about her duties at renovation.

Joellen Bye, a "Historic Interpreter," spotted the image of an old woman in 1984, hair done up in a gray bun, standing on the staircase, looking down at the front room hall. Joellen, at first, thought it might be the residue of last night's dreams infesting her mind (it was, after all, around eight o'clock in the morning), but upon blinking a few times, she realized that the image was not simply a trick of her mind. She took a step forward, perhaps to go up the stairs, perhaps not, but, at any rate, the woman suddenly vanished. It must have left Joellen feeling awed but apprehensive.

There was a second encounter, however, not long after. Joellen claims to have seen the same image of the woman leaving the master bedroom by a side door, going into the servant's passage, as if to make for the stairs. The amazing thing is, is that Joellen (who only spotted the woman's back) was certain that the woman was aware of Joellen's presence, and that she was hurriedly rushing away to avoid an encounter!

After a long while of further disturbances (and, we may assume, some vanished employees), the services of a noted parapsychologist were summoned, a Dr. Tom Greco of Louisville, who, upon immediately entering the home, reported that he was confronted by the specter of the familiar "gray lady" on the first floor staircase, who furthermore beckoned him on to the second floor.

Preferring to go about his duty without the aid of electric lights, Dr. Greco toured the home, noting the presence of sickness and dying that came from the master bedroom, feeling the presence of an elderly woman who must have died there. Perhaps the Gray Lady herself? Who can know for certain?

He further related feelings of sickness, injury, and great consternation and argument over the Civil War. Passing on to the third floor, he found himself in the vicinity of the north children's room. There, he saw (or at least, reported he saw) the figures of two children, a dark haired boy and a blond girl. He never said much about them, except that they must have appeared to him in spirit, for he reportedly said that they acknowledged him with a glance, before disappearing into nothingness.

Next, he came to the south children's bedroom, a room with a door that went into the servant's hallway, and a place that Dr. Greco reported as having intense feelings of terror, hurt, fear, and pain associated with it. Behind the door to the servant's hall, of course (and Dr. Greco had no way of knowing this), was a small, wooden lattice-work cubicle, called the "punishment room," where Cornelia was wont, from time-to-time, to lock the children away for misbehaviors and indiscretions, leaving them cold and hungry in the darkness.

Yes, the Culbertsons were known for the severity of their disciplinary procedures when it came to their children. Their strictness was a thing of gossip. Apparently, they believed the old adage "spare the rod, spoil the child," and took it to heart, brutally.

The doctor cautioned the staff of Culbertson Mansion to avoid working near the "punishment closet," as it acted as a psychic battery of infernal feelings and bad emotions, and was apt to send anyone who spent long hours within the vicinity (and who was even mildly sensitive to such things) into feelings of despair and balefulness. Also, he reportedly asked if Lincoln had ever visited the premises. When told that, no, the famous president had never been known to have visited Culbertson Mansion in his lifetime, Dr. Greco found himself puzzled. Of course, he didn't know that William Culbertson himself was often said to bear a striking resemblance to Abraham Lincoln.

Dr. Greco spoke of many things, but one thing in particular that kept coming home to him was the impression of a family that spent much time in heated arguments. He claimed to hear the echoes of ghostly whispers, half-heard heated discussions, and other tell-tale signs of a family that was often at loggerheads over important matters. And it made a certain sense, even though Dr. Greco could not have known it at the time.

The Culbertsons reportedly had five relatives fighting for the Confederacy during the Civil War…and five for the Union. Further, one of the sons was an alcoholic; one of the daughters was to be married to a Frenchman, and William Culbertson didn't like that one bit. Dr. Greco picked up on snatches of these conversations, bits and pieces of this information, but it meant nothing to him at the time, as he knew nothing about the history of the home.

It was on Halloween of 1985 that the Jaycees decided to utilize Culbertson Mansion for their annual "Spook Run," with two or three days of guests, mostly children, invited in to tour the decorated old manse and thrill and chill to the fake cobwebs, phony ghosts, actors in make-up, trick effects, and chilling stereophonic sounds as they toured the darkened halls. Of course, par for the course, the staff of this particular haunted attraction got some real ghosts thrown in for the bargain.

The lights would mysteriously go on and off, but what was even more bizarre was the crying that was heard mysteriously recorded on one of the Halloween music tapes they were using. Crying that was not, strictly speaking, part of the program[6].

Then, there was the last evening of the haunted house, when the staff of the Culbertson sat down, exhausted at dealing with the parade of little trick or treaters all night, and suddenly began to hear footsteps resounding loudly from the third floor, as if someone was upstairs, walking about excitedly. Since there were only five of them left in the house after clean-up, they realized this was impossible.

Amazingly, the staff had, as a group, stayed one entire night at the old house after work, sleeping in the rooms where ghosts were known to walk. Joellen reportedly settled down to sleep and she began to smell a sickening aroma, the aroma of decay, and it seemed to settle down over her bed. She felt an intense fear grip her, suddenly, and commanded the malodorous phantom (if that's what it truly was) to go away, at once. This seemed to settle the matter, and Joellen was blessed with pleasant rest, afterwards.

The next morning, some staff members awoke complaining about the sounds of heavy doors slamming, and mad footsteps, keeping them up all hours of the night. Others, even those who were in closer proximity to where the noises originated from, said they heard nothing at all.

At times, too, the heavy, rich aroma of pipe tobacco (a common occurrence in haunted houses) is smelt, and the sound of a harsh man's voice can be heard, but never, specifically, what he is saying. Those who have worked at Culbertson Mansion report objects, such as a television, and a massive, ornate harp, moving by themselves. Still others report hearing banging against the walls of the third floor, particularly coming from the area of the "punishment closet."

At other times, strangely, all is quiet. One staff member reported entering a disused storage room, only to find an antique spinning wheel moving by itself. Quite an impossibility when one considered the creaky old contraption actually required quite a bit of raw strength to get it moving. No draft or blast of wayward air could have managed it.

Lisa Higbee, who, amazingly enough, actually took up residence as curator of Culbertson Mansion, related a strange dream she had of getting up from her bed in the middle of the night and going out to the stairs.

On the stairs, balanced precariously on the banister, was the figure of a little girl, dressed in Victorian clothing. In the dream, Lisa warned the small girl to get off of the banister, as she would surely fall to her death. The girl merely smiled, telling her that death might be preferable to the life she was leading at Culbertson Mansion. She then related a tale of woe straight from a Dickens novel: of losing her family in a tragedy and being taken to an orphan's home. Of being selected by the Culbertsons to be their "serving girl," of cruelty and a family that was always quick to bicker and condemn each other. She continued to balance precariously on the edge of the banister, before relating that her name was "Minerva," and that "she would be back."

"I'll be back…and so will you!"

Then the little girl jumped from the banister, and Lisa rushed forward, watching her fall, as if in slow-motion, to her end.

She awoke suddenly. She could hear something stirring out in the hallway, in the darkness. There were footsteps coming toward her, growing louder as they approached her door.

She cowered in bed, in a frenzy of panic. What to do? In vain, she sought to remember a prayer, one that Joellen Bye had taught her, one that she had used to dispel the ghostly footsteps once before, when both of the women had frenziedly sought in vain the empty third floor for a possible source for the phenomenal footsteps and their invisible owner. She couldn't remember the precise prayer, but uttered one of her own. Just in the nick of time, as the steps were now outside her room, they suddenly ceased, right before (we might assume) they entered the room through the solid door.

In 1996, a visiting Dr. Haile stopped by Culbertson Mansion on a whim, knowing nothing about it. He later reported that while studying the ornate work of the floorboards, he caught a quick glance of a gray-clad old woman passing by him. Was this Cornelia, again, leading the way into her beloved abode, which now held her as a sort of spectral prison? Stranger things than even this have been known to haunt our mist-shrouded planet.

A few final notes: All of this material is related in the excellent book *Hoosier Hauntings* by K.T. MacRorie, a book we highly suggest any reader interested in ghostly phenomenon look into obtaining. Mr. MacRorie writes, lovingly, of the grand architecture of the bygone era. ("They sure don't build 'em like this anymore!" you can almost hear him saying, as he walks around, hands on his hips, staring at the occult architecture of that brooding horror of a home.)

Alas, we ourselves are no enthusiast in the subject of Victorian homes, except for how they may, in the space of a century, become repositories for the sorts of phenomenon with which the present volume is chiefly concerned. We'll take his word on the beauty of the place. We are, perhaps, more interested in the architecture of the arcane, for our own part.

As for Lisa Higbee and her macabre dream, upon relating it to Joellen Bye, the woman began to cry. When Lisa asked what was the matter, Joellen flatly stated, "Don't you remember?"

Lisa, in fact did not remember what Cornelia Culbertsons middle name was, but it was the reason for Joellen's tears. And what was her middle name? Haven't you already guessed?

It was *Minerva*.

William Culbertson had several wives before Cornelia. She must have come to the household very young. It seems, in time, she learned the casual cruelty of the Culbertson ways.

(One wonders how many nights she spent in the "punishment closet" herself, as a girl.)

As to her promise that "I'll be back…and so will you!" implying, perhaps, that Minerva and Lisa would be meeting in dreams for many disturbing nights hence, Lisa Higbee has never as yet been forthcoming concerning the validity of this statement.

We may allow her some leeway, perhaps, in this regard.

23

Waltzing Matilda

George Dewees was, by all accounts, a miserable, two-fisted *sonofabitch* who once shot a man in the back in New Orleans for cheating in a card game. He was also, by the standards of early nineteenth-century Indiana, a wealthy man of taste and cultivation. His monument to posterity, the Preston House, is built in the manner of the august Old South, and cannot fail to impress anyone fortunate enough to stop by for a visit.

Dewees was well-known around town as a sullen blackguard; consequently, was not well-liked by anyone, and was a constant center of speculation and gossip. His only companion, a long-suffering wife by the name of Matilda, was little seen about town, but was known to bear up under a continual stream of physical and mental abuse from her short-tempered spouse. Finally, she disappeared, and was never known outside of the curious whispers concerning George Dewees and his unsavory life, again.

When Dewees died, in 1834, it was soon rumored that Matilda, who arose like a phoenix from the ashes of distant recall, had been the victim of an accident. Or an illness. Or, most likely, foul play, considering the stormy, violent temper of her husband. A story soon began circulating that George Dewees had murdered his wife in a fit of rage after she threatened to finally leave him. But who can credit the veracity of such claims after so long a period of time?

What is certain is that, that unhappy soul, apparently, has seen fit to continue her somber perambulations around the Preston House, contravening the generally accepted logic that time heals all wounds. Or so it is claimed by those who have reported the chilling cold spots, aberrant, spectral mist, and weird, otherworldly illumination that stalks the corridors of Preston House. Legend has it that the body of the aggrieved Matilda is bricked up in the large fireplace in the east room of the old house, the other fireplaces having cupboards on both sides, while the fireplace in the east room, curiously, has none.

Whether this be true or not, what is undoubtedly true is the odd psychic sensations that accompany many visitors through the aged old hallways and vacant rooms. In 1985, the Vigo Preservation Alliance

held a tour through the home, making sure, for publicity sake, to bring along the expertise of a local, reputable psychic.

The psychic allegedly knew nothing of the old place, yet, correctly named the specter of "Matilda" as the resident specter, and furthermore elaborated that Matilda was intrigued to find her home being visited by so many unfamiliar faces.

Incidentally, it is not only the interior of the Preston House that finds itself the habitation of spooks and phantoms, but the very grounds of the old place itself have a startling history as a repository of pain, anguish, and the malignant energy of untimely death.

George Dewees, who was himself a slave owner, could have no way of knowing that one day his stately home would be utilized to transport slaves, via the "Underground Railroad," to freedom and relative security in Canada. Of course, since assisting escaped slaves was illegal, the operation was entirely clandestine (and extremely dangerous, for slave and abolitionist alike). Thus, the cellar of the Preston House became a part of a system of tunnels wherein escaped slaves could be kept until they could be smuggled farther along the network.

Unfortunately, this practice was to be brought to an abrupt halt when a portion of the basement, for unknown reasons, collapsed, trapping a good number of men, women, and children below, in a suffocating darkness from which there was no escape. The abolitionists, for their part, were powerless to do anything, for to rescue the dying slaves would have meant digging up a huge portion of the earth, which no doubt would have aroused the suspicions of the local law enforcement and ended whatever usefulness the abolitionists would be able to afford their movement. It was finally decided that rescuing the trapped slaves was too risky, and they were left to a death more hideous than any of us can possibly imagine.

To this day, there are those who swear that they can, some lonely nights, hear the anguished cries and moans of the dying come, like a whisper from the netherworld, floating across the grounds of the old place.

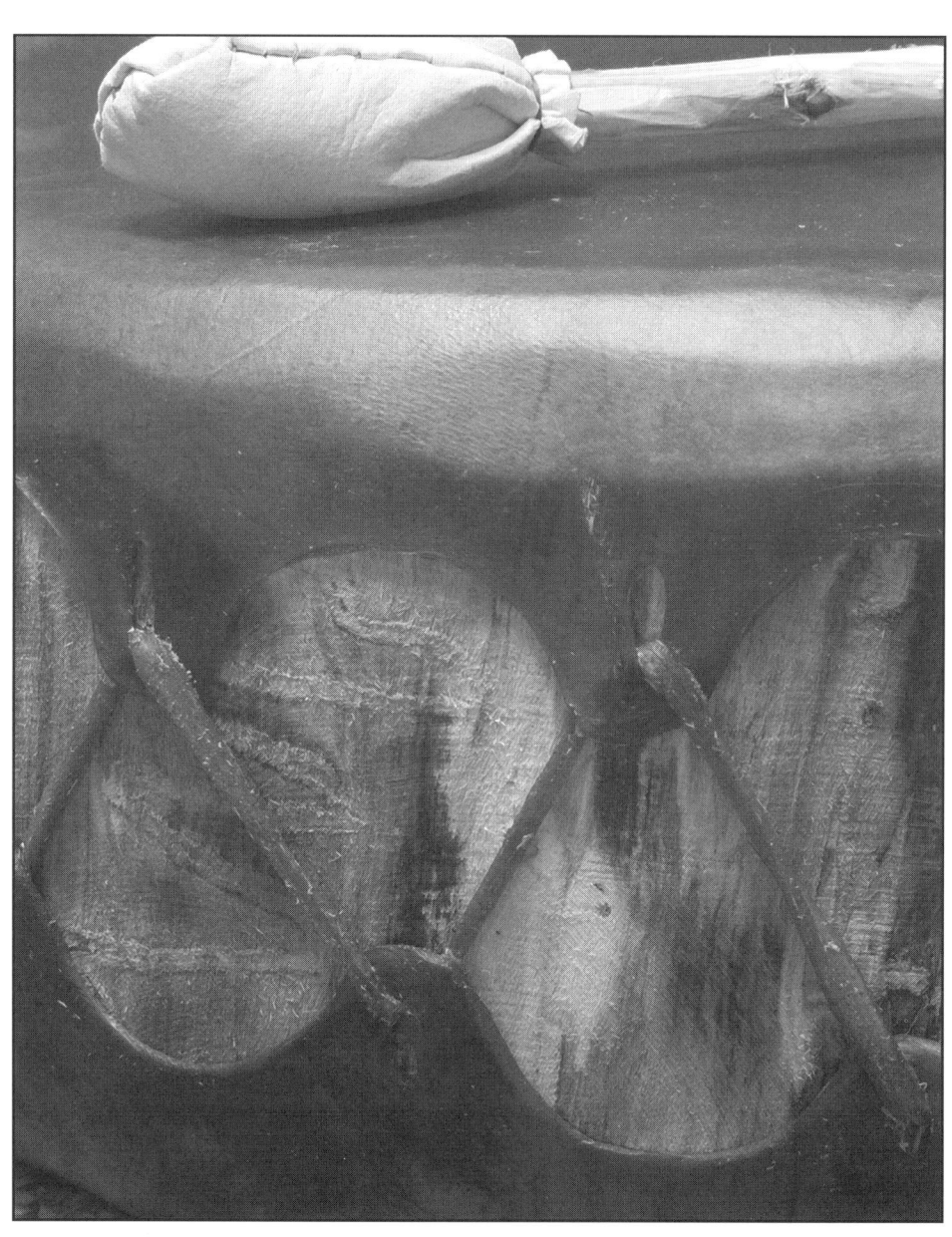

24

Black Rock
and Mourning Glory

There was a time, before the coming of the White Man and his religion, when the land that comprises the State of Indiana was ruled by the Native American and his God, the Great White Spirit, who reigned over a court of wild, supernatural personages and mischievous spirits.

Such spirits were the stuff of everyday experience for the Native American, who knew them and accepted them as easily as he accepted that Fall is followed by Winter, and night by day. Such manifestations of the unity between matter and energy, between life and death, were commonplace to those people who relied on the traditions of their ancestors, and their own personal "inner vision" to guide them through the pathways of life.

Thus such stories as we are to relate here are by no means exceptional, but prove the rule.

One such tale concerns the fate of an Indian maiden who was suspected of causing the death of Chief Monoquet. When she somehow discovered the news of her suspected guilt, she grew terrified, realizing that the punishment for this would surely be a hideous death. She fled into the darkness of the forest, alone, hoping to make her way back to her tribe in the north. However, she would never leave the woods of Kosciosko County ever again. In time, two young braves would track her down in the forest, and avenge what they presumed to be her murder of Chief Monoquet.

They may have tortured her; certainly her death was painful and gruesome. The accounts of Native Americans torturing their enemies are graphic, intensely disturbing stuff. Such a death would invite, it would seem, a restless, ill-fated spirit to wander the woods and back roads, in search of some meaning.

And so it is that the ghost of the Indian Maiden is said to be seen "just south of Leesburg, on the road to Clunette." But she has been

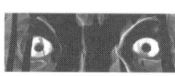

reported in other places as well. She appears to be lost, frightened, forever journeying back to her people, her tribe, on a quest from peril that will never be consummated with arrival.

"Polly Pratt" (a woman who may or may not have been a complete invention of local folklore) was said to be a hated and despised figure in old South Bend, even more so because she was French, and did not get on well with American settlers. She did, however, strike up a curious comradeship with a tribe of Native Americans, who, once they had come to town to trade their pelts for goods (usually whiskey), proceeded to Polly Pratt's place, to imbibe themselves and have a riotous time. It is said that Polly was very accommodating to her Indian friends, and was quite pleased that their presence was enough to drive away any neighbors that may come calling. Not that any, apparently, ever did.

It is said, in legend, that one night, the Native American tribe camped out in Polly Pratt's yard became more drunk and exuberant than usual. They were plotting an uprising, to kill all the White settlers (except, of course, for Polly), and they began to wave their daggers around viciously. It was this throwing around of knives that led to the tragedy that came later, as one of the braves was cut, accidentally, quite badly. There was nothing that could be done for him. He died.

It was soon after that the Native Americans disappeared from Polly Pratt's premises; so too, did Polly Pratt. Perhaps she was adopted by tribe, or perhaps she simply moved on after the tragedy. Perhaps something more sinister became of her, but, whatever it was, she was not seen in South Bend, again.

The young brave who was killed, however, is said to still haunt the trees (we suppose he crouched in them, as if on lookout) in Chapin Park. Perhaps he is looking for his tribe to come and claim him once more for a rousing game of drinking and knife-throwing, ensconced in their encampment at the doorstep of Polly Pratt.

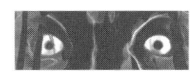

Certainly the strangest Native American ghost story to come from Indiana is that of the Ghost of Black Rock, related by a mysterious journalist known only as "Morning Glory" to his readers.

It was in the *Lafayette Morning Journal* of August 1890 where the story was first told.

Black Rock, a geological formation of occult significance, where Native American tribes of three states (Indiana, Illinois, and Ohio) all met for council, stands like a silent, rocky sentinel twelve miles southwest of Lafayette, and is reportedly the burying place for a long-hidden treasure. (Did it perhaps belong to Blackbeard?)

Deep caves are said to go down into the murky, serpent-haunted recesses of Black Rock, and it is in these caverns that the treasure is said to be hidden. However, no one has ever dared to come forth and explore the caverns in search of it. For, if they did, they would meet the Ghost of Black Rock, and something terrible might happen to them, as a result.

Our intrepid journalist, "Morning Glory" was however too eager a reporter to turn down such an incredible tale, so, while sleeping one night at a fishing camp on the banks of the river, he kept watch for the tell-tale opalescent light that signaled the coming of the Ghost, and, summoning his comrades, he set out in a fishing boat toward the light, in hopes of securing the interview of his career.

The intrepid journalist and his somewhat less enthusiastic crew started off in their boat, singing a merry song, apparently, to bolster their bravado, but soon faltering in their joviality as they approached the solemn, ominous Rock. Soon, they made their landing, and Morning Glory enquired of his friends if any of them cared to accompany him up the rock, in search of the Ghost.

"No," replied one. "But I'll stay here if I can until you come back. If you ever do come back."

Undeterred, the bold young man began his ascent. It was tough going in the dark, and he soon found himself slipping and exhausted, but finally, he made his way to the strange, luminescent light at the mouth of a dark cave. There, before his unbelieving eyes, sat a skeletal horror of a man, a Native American chief, with his chin resting on his skeletal old hand. He must have looked, for all the world, like that famous statue of The Thinker.

At the approach of company, however, the Ghost soon sprang to life, roaring at the intruder to state his business. Morning Glory (a man, quite obviously, made of some very stern stuff), replied that he had come a long way for an exclusive interview with the Ghost of Black Rock.

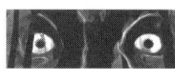

According to Morning Glory, the Ghost, far from being offended by the offer, soon found himself confessing the strange, poignant tale of his life to this complete stranger, who had just a short while ago sailed up in a fishing boat.

He claimed to have been a powerful chief in the year 900, when the river was mighty and filled with canoes, his tribe having been a massive nation unto themselves at the time. He claimed to have been a wild, fierce hunter, and to have killed many men, but was now paying for it by being condemned to spend his eternity poised as a sentinel at Black Rock.

He said:

> *"The meanest creature of the Great Spirit has the same right to life that you have, and beware how you take it, if you would be happy hereafter. I slaughtered ruthlessly anything that stood in my way, man or beast, and I am being punished for it. I was finally killed myself in a battle over yonder with poisoned arrows. And I discovered that this dying is no fun.*
> *"The tribes assembled and they buried my body with ceremonies befitting a great chief. I watched it all poised in the air, a free spirit, and they gave me a send-off that was very gratifying to my pride. They danced and feasted for three days, and the quantity of maize and raw dog that was consumed was astonishing."*

He went on to describe how he had visited the "Happy Hunting Grounds," but how he wasn't contented there, as the game was too tame and docile. He further told Morning Glory that he descended, often, to the Underworld, to take care of things for Satan, when Satan was away, doing the "devil's work" at camp meetings and in churches.

His most poignant story involved his eternal vigilant wait for his lost bride, Laska, who was riding behind him when he was felled by a poisoned arrow. She was in "Devachan" now, but would soon return to earth so they could be reunited. Poetically, he referred to her as, " ...sister of the stars, and the night wind..."

A sudden burst of emotion from the old spirit, and a wave of the arms, finally sent the courage of Morning Glory running for cover, and the bold young reporter was scampering close behind. The Ghost had, finally, managed to frighten him away, but not before he got the story of his life. Or so it appeared, at least.

Why he chose to publish under the particular moniker of "Morning Glory" is entirely unknown, but perhaps "Mourning Glory" would have been a more fitting sobriquet. At any rate, the story quickly caught fire, and not a few brave souls must have wrestled within themselves for the courage to either journey, by night and boat, to Black Rock, to see the old Chief for themselves, and perhaps get an interview with the ghost.

As for Chief Black Rock, whither went his spirit, none can say, but we have a feeling that, some night soon, you may see the opalescent, unearthly glow emanating from Black Rock. And you too may wonder. And you may dare….

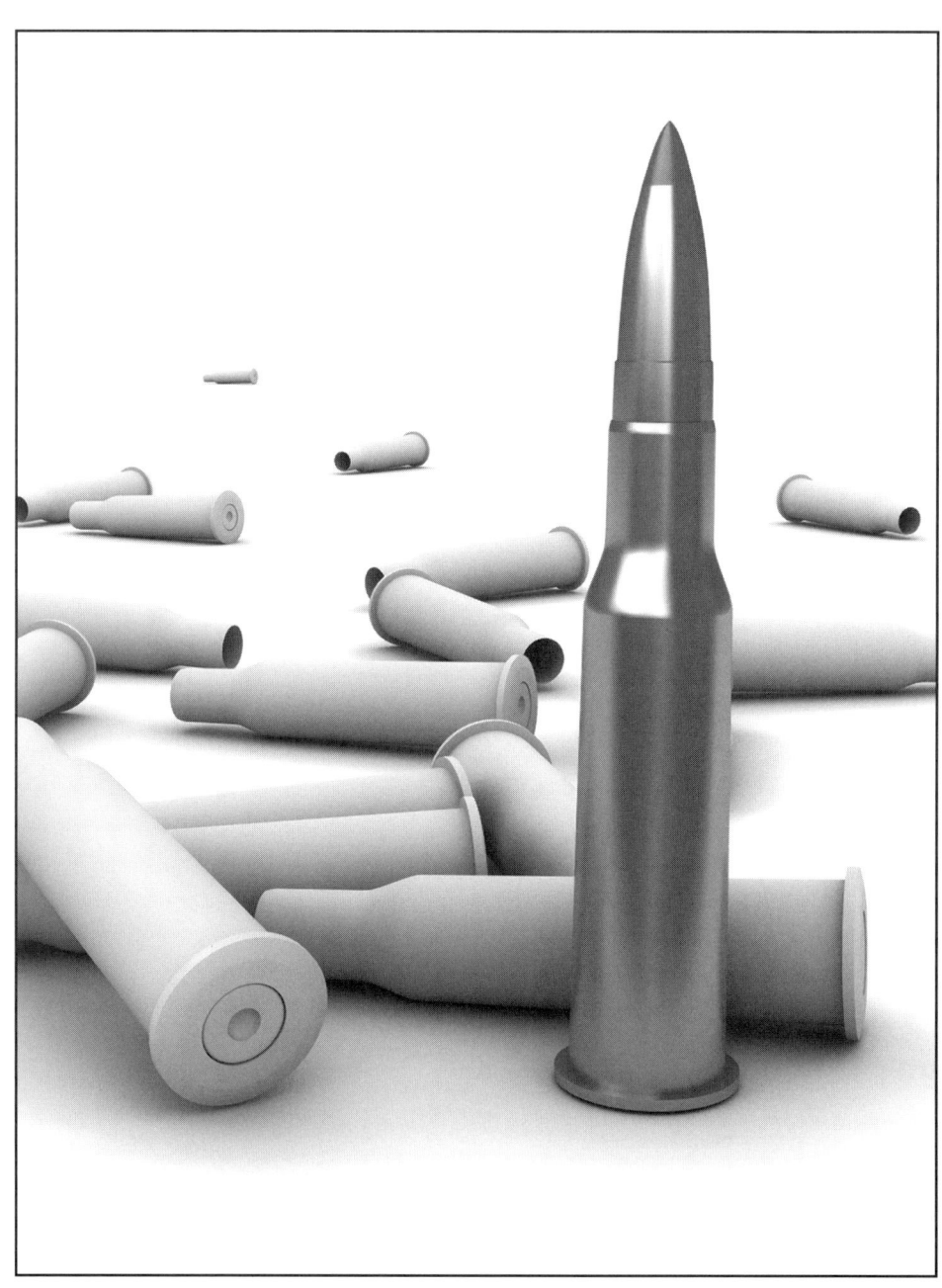

25

Wild Witches and Death Tokens

The idea that death, that greatest and most fearsome (and most certain) of all common human experiences could be foretold by some event or omen that occurs in the environment of the mortally afflicted is one that seems to be common to mankind. Indeed, the idea of the fatal omen is suggested even in Shakespeare, where a doomed Caesar is warned to "beware the Ides of March!" amidst a general tumult of inexplicable aerial signs and wonders. Such ideas were common to the ancient peoples of Rome, who employed a special class of augers to interpret the random flights of birds or the convulsive entrails of a disemboweled animal.

The idea that the future can be divined, then, in the smallest minutiae (if but one knows how to read the various symbols!) is what sits at bottom of many a carefully-considered teacup, or atop the tables of so many shufflers of Tarot cards and other such "fortune telling" amusements.

What, though, are we to make of the omen or "death token" that does not sit, placidly, like some obscure ideogram, waiting for the elect soothsayer to ferret it out of hiding and interpret it, but comes, as if sent by supernatural telegram, to bother and confuse those clueless souls that were not even bothering to look for it?

In Indiana, we have such a tradition of mysterious "death tokens," a few of which are related here, for your general amusement and wonder.

One of the most common of all death tokens is, apparently, three mysterious knocks on the door immediately preceding the departure of a loved one. One cannot say why, specifically, three knocks would do it, except that death in families are always expected to come in threes, and thus, one supposes it makes a sort of macabre sense. Alternately, three stout raps against a headboard (for those that still have headboards) are expected to signal the oncoming or incipient death of a loved one.

A more logical death token would be the stopping of a clock or watch, as, symbolically, the stopping of a timepiece owned by a particular individual is a metaphor both for the passing of time and the inevitability of

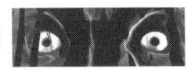

the end of all things. Everything is impermanent, transient. Time is an illusion just as much as life, and nothing lasts forever.

Sobering thoughts, to be sure.

The falling of a portrait upon the floor may herald an oncoming demise, as may the shattering of a mirror. Does the mirror have to, in some way, be connected to the person who is about to die? Does it have to belong to them, or have belonged to them? No one can say for certain.

Even a broken dish can herald onrushing mortality. We suppose if it was the favorite eating dish of the person who has, lately, become the target of the Reaper's attentions, we could understand. However, the information we have forthcoming doesn't distinguish if this is, in fact, the case. Suffice it to say the human mind can make connections and draw coincidental strands together to form a complete whole when the need arises, or the amount of stress or grief is sufficient to do so.

Or, perhaps, in some way unknown to man, the small, seemingly insignificant events of our lives do have hidden patterns, draw unmistakably arcane and subtle lines between seemingly random occurrences, and can be read as a sort of "small print" edition of that Which Is To Be. Hence, the future can be read in a strange configuration of tea leaves, a deck of common playing cards, or the steaming entrails of a slaughtered animal.

Speaking of which, the lonely flight of mysterious bird could also be interpreted as an omen of death, as in a story related in the book *Hoosier Folklore*, by Ronald L. Baker (no relation to the present author). Mr. Baker relates the story of a Mr. and Mrs. Kinzer, who, one fine and seemingly average morning long ago, sat around the kitchen, when the elderly Mr. Kinzer suddenly and inexplicable reached over, as if to grab for something on the table.

Since there was nothing, seemingly, within his grasp, his wife asked him what on earth it was he thought he was doing, to which he replied that he was simply grabbing at a large white bird that had flown into the room and settled upon the kitchen table. His wife, thinking he must be going daft, urged him to finish breakfast that they both might go out to the barn and complete some morning chores.

In due time, they both were in the barn, in different spots, but, unfortunately for Mrs. Kinzer, she suddenly, and quite unexpectedly, dropped stone dead from a heart attack, due possibly to the exertion of her labors. She was gone by the time Mr. Kinzer could even get to her. A sad tale, certainly, and most assuredly Mr. Kinzer never forgot his strange morning vision of the elusive white bird.

Other meaningful death tokens have included spectral flames, hooded wraiths (we'll be meeting some of these shortly), and, of course, dreaming of caskets, that final vehicle of bereavement which carries the consigned remains to their place of eternal repose.

Mark Twain, in a very famous vision, is said to have seen the body of his brother laid out in a fine metal casket, with a bouquet of roses placed upon his chest, and a single white carnelian placed there later, by a mysterious woman in black.

This vision came to him in the midst of a feverish dream. Later, when his brother was killed during a steamship explosion (a common enough occurrence in those days), Twain was amazed to find that a number of sympathetic women scrounged together the money for a truly magnificent burial, complete with heavy metal casket. As Twain entered the room, unbelievingly, a woman dressed in black mourning attire crept in, placing a single white carnelian in the center of the floral arrangement in the young man's dead grasp. He must have felt faint, after witnessing that display.

President Abraham Lincoln likewise had a disturbing dream wherein he went downstairs and crept through a deserted Whitehouse, only to find a sentry standing guard at the entrance to a room below. Suddenly, he realized that there was a funeral going on in the next room. He asked the young man who had died.

"The President, Sir. He was killed by an assassin."

Of course, Lincoln was later shot dead at Ford's Theatre by the crazed John Wilkes Boothe, who jumped from the theatre balcony screaming, "Sic semper tyrannis!" (Or, "thus always to tyrants"), before falling to the stage, breaking his leg, and dying later in a confrontation in front of an old barn where he was in hiding.

Lincoln was a much-hated man, and must have known there were no end to the violent, revenge-filled men that would like to do harm to him. This undoubtedly colored his waking moments, as well as his sleeping. Still, coincidence can hardly account for every incident of precognition or strange omens of the future can it?

We've gone far a field of Old Indiana, we fear, so for the moment, we will leave portents of death and omens of destruction behind in favor of profiling our local witches. Yes, you read that last part correctly. Indiana was once rife with those haggard old crones of lore that practiced the black arts, poisoned livestock, ruined the weather, rotted crops in the field and fruit on the vine, and generally made life an unpleasant hell for whoever raised their ire.

When we use the term "witches" here, we are in fact NOT referring to Wicca, or any modern practitioners of the ancient nature-worshipping religions that follow the path laid out by Gerald Gardner or other individuals who have sought to restore the traditional worship of the Goddess and her Horned Consort. These individuals practice a pagan rite that is both beneficial, harmless, and takes as its credo "As Ye Harm No One, Do As Ye Will." It is also growing in popularity as with generations

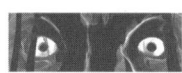

of disaffected college-age young people, who may be alienated from the traditional religious values of their parents and are perhaps seeking their roots in a romanticized, pre-Christian past that is part fantasy and part truth. We wish them all the happiness they can conjure.

Our witches, in fact, really are devious old crones that poison wells and do other dreadful and nasty things, and they exist in tales such as the following.

Once, there was a woman in Giro, Indiana (described as a small German community that was as stolid and conservative in its ways as it was in its superstitions), who was busily churning butter, but was finding herself having little luck. For hours she worked the churn, but nothing came out, and finally, she turned to her husband, exclaiming, "Some witch has her foot in my churn, but I'll soon take care of her!" Off she flew to the fireplace, grabbing herself a hot iron, and dropping it inside the churn. A piercing, scalding sort of sound could be heard to faintly erupt, but it was all the same to the woman, for now she had all the thick, rich butter that she wanted.

It was only the next day that she went round the neighborhood to have a chat with "Mrs. Jones." When she got there, she found the poor woman to be in an uncommonly sorry state as she was limping to the door—with a bandaged foot!

"What happened to your foot, Mrs. Jones?" the woman, asked, suspiciously.

"Oh dearie, I've burned it most terribly!"

Of course, the reader is invited to draw their own conclusions.

Of course, witches were famous for always going about "hexing" things (still are, as far as that goes). In one particular story, related amazingly enough, in a more modern setting, involves a particularly nasty-looking crone with an apple orchard and an astoundingly mentally unstable daughter, reputedly that way because she'd witnessed her brother-in-law murder her own sister.

This woman owned an orchard, and when a neighboring black farmer happened to let a cow roam free and into the orchard one day, it so incensed the old witch that she went, forthwith, and placed a curse on his well, causing the water to go sour. Or, perhaps it was all a coincidence. For centuries, hysterical bigots accused Jewish people of doing the same thing to *their* wells.

The supposed hex involved throwing a penny down the well. Ergo, the treatment (known to the old black man, supposedly, because he was well versed in the lore of his own Caribbean heritage) was to heat a nickel, and throw it in the well. One supposes some words might have been uttered back and forth between these two humble wonder workers, but who really knows.

Apparently, this did the trick. What retribution the old man might have sent the old crone is not recorded, nor can be assumed for lack of verifiable evidence, anecdotal or otherwise.

A most frightening tale of a witch involves a Southern Indiana man who was, apparently, sleeping with one! He was the owner of a grist mill, a particularly successful enterprise from where he stood, but he had a hell of time keeping employees on hand. It was the mystifying "cat," a strange creature of a mysteriously feline shape and piercing, demonic cries that haunted the place at night, that made it impossible for any sane man (even the hardiest of them) to stand to be near the place after the sun set.

Not being one to be suckered into believing in the supernatural, the man decided for himself to wait up one lonely night, when the moon was full, to see if he could catch a glimpse of it. Whatever IT happened to be.

"Probably just a raccoon," he may have snorted to himself. But, at any rate, he took his gun along with him, just in case.

Selecting a secret vantage point to which he could get a clear view of the grounds as they slumbered under the moonlight, he seated himself against the stump of an old tree, with his rifle ready, and a sharp knife thrust into his waistband.

He must have nodded off at some point, but it was not long before he began to hear some rustling in the growth beyond, coming up the bank. He stirred himself, and, suddenly, saw two piercing red eyes glowering out at him in the dark. A huddled shape began to slink forward—a filthy, feline shape that resembled no cat he had ever seen before. He aimed, dead center between the fiery eyes, and the thing let loose a wail that could have stripped paint from the side of a barn had there been a barn handy. He clicked the trigger—nothing. The rifle mysteriously had jammed. He suddenly threw it down in terror, preparing to make a mad dash for it, when the thing leapt, its claws no doubt bared and its fangs dripping. He reached for his knife, slashing out madly, striking the thing in the paw.

It must have been a lucky blow, for the thing slunk backward, suddenly disappearing in a cloud of smoky vapor. He crept forward on trembling legs, looking down at an inky pool with a twitching, black paw in the center.

Then, suddenly, that too vanished in a cloud of dusty smoke.

He wandered home, making it to his front door by daybreak. He was confronted by his daughter, who had obviously not slept a wink.

"Oh, Father, it's terrible! Mother got her hand cut off last night. We bandaged it as best we could, but she's upstairs, and Doc says she's lost a lot of blood."

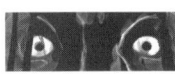

Of course, not all "witches" can be interpreted as being "bad," or having malicious intent. A very good witch to have around is a "water witch," or, more popularly, a "dowser," a tradition that has a long and venerable history in Indiana and all across the Midwest.

A dowser will take a stick of forked wood (or, sometimes, a pair of metal dowsing rods) and will attempt to locate water in hopes of digging a needed well—although people have been known to "dowse" for other things, as well, such as gold or buried treasure.

Dowsers are said to have electricity in their body, or often talk of "spirits" entering their arms. The stories of dowsers walking around rather madly with forked sticks and mysteriously finding underground veins of water where none were suspected of being, are numerous and plentiful, and all rather too much to go into here. Other famous "folk remedies" of the Hoosier state include domestic "witches" that could cure warts (the cures for warts are, seemingly, endless), as well as stop bleeding, cure ulcers, remove blemishes, and perform any other number of small, helpful homemade spells and suchlike contrivances. It is not within the scope of the present volume to catalog them all, or even a fraction of them, although we found the idea of the "fire letter" (a letter, the possession of which, guaranteed that a home would never burn down) rather intriguing, and the idea that walking back and forth in front of the dwelling while reciting the contents of the letter (the "magic spell"[7] as it were), is as much a part of the tradition of "speaking into power" the Will of the Magician as any high ceremonial magic ever enacted over bell, book, and candle.

We have time for one last tale of witchery, and it is an important one. Perhaps we should preface it by stating that it has been reputed that silver bullets (much like the fabled werewolf) are supposed to stop the offending witch dead in her tracks.

Of course, being shot by a silver bullet would damn well stop anyone dead in their tracks, but I suppose that is a moot point.

We do suggest to the reader that, should they suspicion their next door neighbor of being a witch—though she be a hooked-nose old crone with a face full of warts, a tall, black cap, and the voice of a sepulchral revenant—it is far better to verify first that, indeed, she be a broomstick-riding, devil-worshipping, frequenter of midnight bacchanals before any amount of blessed silver is obtained and fashioned into the requisite silver bullet. Better safe than sorry.

A man named Jabe, who was apparently suffering the effects of a debilitating brain disease, was said to be "hag ridden," or, in other words, of having an invisible witch sitting on his chest, torturing him. He was tied to the posts of his bed, but his ravings got to be so unbearable that a local "witch" (or rather, a woman steeped in the old folk traditions and gifted in the psychic arts) was consulted. She immediately prescribed a remedy designed to cure and kill, in the same measure.

Soot from the chimney of the afflicted man was gathered, and a brown paper was inscribed with the image of the "witch" or the hooded "old crone" that was so tormenting him. At least, we assume they went by his descriptions when painting this particular gruesome likeness.

It was then wrapped up into the hole of an old tree, and one of the relatives of the man, a keen shot, aimed a rifle at the trunk and blasted forth with the aforementioned silver bullet (where said bullet was obtained, and how, on such short notice, is a matter of debate and speculation).

Having thus completed the working of the "spell" the small group of family members went back upstairs to the room of the afflicted man, and found themselves amazed at the contented smile that spread across his now happy visage.

The "Old hag" was apparently now dead.

Unfortunately for the family, so was their tormented kin.

One should not forget, beyond all of these stories, that for centuries, belief in witches and their power were quite real to most people, and this belief consigned thousands to torture and flames as the "Witch Hysteria" swept through much of Europe. Men, women, and children were broken on the rack, tortured with spikes and hot pincers, made to confess to absurd charges and, if they did not confess, tortured and killed anyway. They were, most often, consigned to the flames, burned at the stake in a hellish death that must have sent psychic terror cavorting down through the ages with piercing moans and shuddering screams of wretchedness.

The instruments of this barbarity are still extant, and are on display in many museums—a testament to man's inhumanity to man. It was a monstrous, terrible thing that occurred during those Dark Ages. We must be ever-vigilant in the face of such hysterical persecutions of "heretics," whoever they may be.

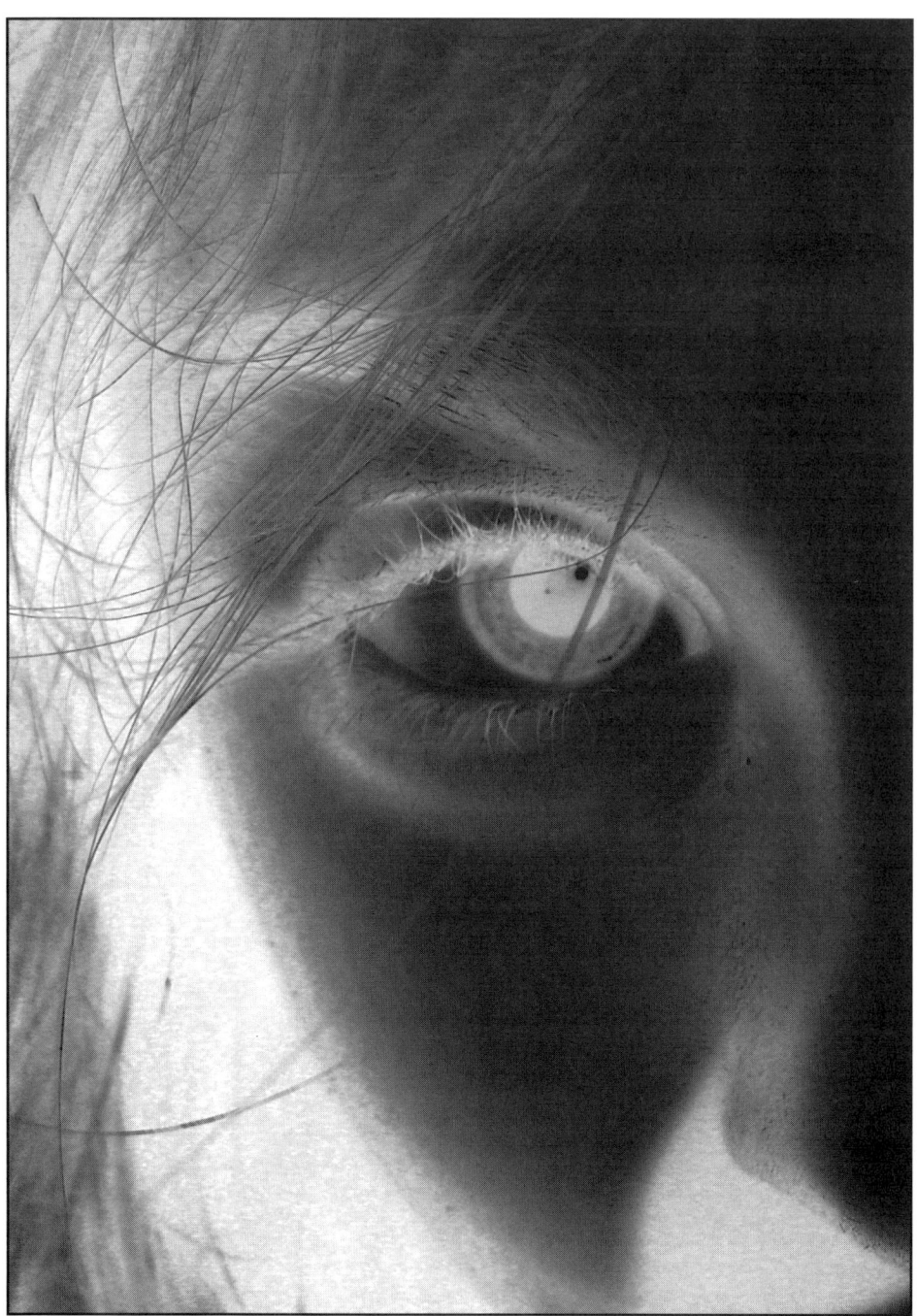

26

The Arrival
and the Reunion

We come, thus, to the end of our sordid tour of the scary hinterlands of Hoosier experience, and find ourselves, amazingly enough, back where we began. On that same lonely street, with two mystified onlookers gazing upward at the disappearing object, fading to a small red pinpoint in the distance.

"What in the hell was that?"

"That," began the boy, his voice a slow mixture of astonishment and nervous mockery, "was someone a little off course. Like about thirteen million light-years."

"Oh, be still," said the aunt. But they were both starting to feel the chill of the night.

"Maybe we better get inside," suggested the boy. Privately, he was thinking: *I don't want to be standing here if they decide to come back.*

"Yeah, maybe you're right," said the boy's aunt. But they went slowly back to the apartment, on knees that felt rubbery. They both felt surprisingly sedate, still, all things considered, yet that indelible image was burned into the mind of the boy as surely as if it had been implanted there by hypnotic suggestion.

They both felt oddly numb, confused; experts might say they were both experiencing a state of shock. As they went through the door of the apartment, the boy's mother exclaimed, "Where in the world have you two been? I fell asleep waiting, and when I woke up I realized you'd been gone for over two hours. I was going to call the police."

Both the boy and the aunt looked at each other, and the boy suddenly said, "Mom, you're not going to believe what I have to tell you. But we saw something strange out there..."

He trailed off, uncertain of how to proceed.

"What do you mean, 'You saw something strange?'"

"It was a flying saucer!" He suddenly blurted out. "Or, I guess it wasn't really a saucer. It was more like a giant cigar. Mom, it was the most incredible thing I've ever seen in my entire life."

Suddenly, the strange haze seemed to wear off of both of them a bit, and the aunt, a little sheepishly said, " He's not making it up. It…I can't explain what the hell that thing was. It came up from over the field across the street."

The mother seemed a little suspicious, but having heard her sister verify the story, must have realized that, essentially, both of them were telling the truth as they understood it.

"Are you sure it wasn't a flare or something? Maybe a shooting star?"

"Oh no, Ma! This thing was incredible. Huge. Lights on both ends, and flashing on top. It went up and didn't make any noise. Then it burst into red light, and whisked away. Quicker than sh--!"

"Watch your mouth!" The mother warned.

"Sorry! Quicker than anything I've ever seen before in my entire life! And it didn't make any noise. None at all."

The boy's mother looked at her sister. She could tell, faintly, that her sister was disturbed by the whole affair, and maybe even a little embarrassed. She said, "Is he being straight about all of this."

Reluctantly, the boy's aunt said, "Yes…it, it isn't something I think I could ever explain. Tell you the truth, I don't believe it's anything that came from this world."

It was strange, the boy's mother thought, to hear her sister speak like that. Suddenly, her sister turned around and looked at the clock above the television set on the wall.

"I don't know where in the world the time got to tonight. I guess maybe we got so excited about that thing we just…lost track of time."

The boy yawned loudly, and sat down heavily in a chair, his head falling over into his chest.

"I think I need to get someone home and in bed. Terri, I'll call you tomorrow. Try not to have any more 'close encounters' while you guys are out walking, okay? It seems like I've been waiting for hours."

On the ride home, the boy sleepily looked out the window, resting his head on the cold glass and watching the stars whiz by above the chilly tree tops. Inside, he wrestled with the reality of what he had just seen, and the sensible part of himself that said such things couldn't be, that they only existed in the realm of science fiction movies and make believe. He searched for an explanation for the phenomenon. The search was, however, in vain.

By the time his head hit the pillow, he had virtually eliminated every possibility except shared hallucination. And he didn't properly understand how two people could suddenly have the same hallucination.

He was a smart lad, and he knew that he had encountered, in the space of one evening, a genuine "unknown."

He was, of course, troubled by strange dreams that night, However, he had always been a rather unusual boy, and he had often been plagued by strange dreams and curious fancies.

He had also had a number of disquieting experiences in his life, experiences that he usually kept buried in his conscious mind, only ruminating on them in some strange reveries, or being assaulted by them as they swam up, unexpectedly, like gaping, hungry fish, into the shallow waters of his immediate concentration.

One of the earliest of these memories, he was sometimes convinced, was of actually leaving his body and ascending toward a glowing tunnel that had developed in his bedroom ceiling. As a child, he had been plagued with pneumonia, and was often bed-ridden and very ill. Doctors, at one point, feared that he might not live to see another birthday, and his mother, distraught and traumatized by this prospect, was careful to keep constant vigil over him, day and night.

One night, as he lay in his little bed, with his mother sitting beside him, fading in and out of sleep, he suddenly felt himself began to lift above his ailing body. It was amazing, and he at first felt panic, looking over at his mother, who had curled up beside him in the little bed. Above him, in the swirling darkness of the ceiling, he began to see a smoky light grow, brighter and brighter, until it formed itself into a strange tunnel. The child began to panic as he felt himself floating upward, and he struggled against the magnetic pull of the light. Suddenly, in the midst of the bizarre tunnel that had seemed to open up into conventional reality, he thought he could make out the form of a figure, beckoning to him.

It seemed to be the figure of a little girl, a dark silhouette against the blinding light. She seemed to be wearing a short, old-fashioned dress, and pigtails. Suddenly, she reached out with a skinny arm, inviting him into the light, most likely forevermore.

Apparently though, it was not his time, as the boy felt his spirit turn in the air, and begin to drift back to the strange lump beneath the covers that he knew, in one second of sheer terror and wonder, was his own body. He seemed to reenter that body through the forehead, and gradually came back to wakefulness. Soon, he was drifting back to sleep, assured that his strange experience had been nothing more than a disturbing feverish dream.

It was not many years later, when his family was driving back on a long, lonesome stretch of highway from Texas to Indiana, that another strange experience seemed to mark itself upon the fabric of his childhood mind.

He had been lying in the backseat of his parents car, snoozing, fading in and out of dreams. In truth, the young boy had been very depressed; his father had joined the military, and the family was forced to move, yet again, away from the boy's grandparents and his close, immediate family, to a strange new environment.

It was dark and moonless as the family drove down the long, duty road toward their new home, and the boy couldn't help but peep out at the vast expanse of stars that shined in the hot Texas sky, just beyond the comforting barrier of the back window. His parents, exhausted already from their long trip, spoke softly in the front seat, in deference to their dozing child as he lay on his back behind them.

Suddenly, the boy felt a strange light play against his half-closed lids, and a bizarre airplane seemed to glide slowly past, visible behind the car through the back window. It was very powerfully lit, he thought, and moved slower than any airplane he had ever before witnessed. He wondered exactly what sort of aircraft it might represent, and thought to ask his father (who was an enthusiast when it came to aviation), but decided to try and resume his nap. Then, a sort of strange shock jolted him awake. His eyes flew open, and he sat up, scanning the back window for a sign of the mysterious craft, which had now seemingly vanished.

He was certain that there was something wrong with that particular airplane. To begin with, he was certain no ordinary airplane would be lit up in such a strange, shifting pattern of brilliant lights.

Secondly, he had never before seen an airplane that was perfectly round.

He started to say something to his parents, to tell them of the bizarre object he had seen flying out the back window, but then thought better of it. They would never believe him, he knew. They would dismiss it as the fanciful dream of a small boy, just woken from a fitful sleep.

He lay back down, suddenly feeling a strange sort of sedate calm steal over his body. Blackness followed the closing of his eyes, and the rest was momentary forgetfulness.

He was roused to wakefulness in what seemed a short time later. He groggily tried to shake confusion from his mind, but he realized that something was wrong with his parents. His father was yelling, and his mother was crying in the passenger seat, asking, in a terrified, trembling voice, "David, David, what is it? What's happening?"

"Brenda, I don't know! The headlights seem to keep going out!"

"We'd better pull over!"

Indeed, as the boy sat hunched forward between the driver and the passenger seat, he could see that the road ahead would go from heavy illumination to pitch blackness, and back again, as they sped forward. The last thing he remembered was his father bringing the car to a screeching halt at the side of the road, or perhaps pulling off onto a side road. He could never remember afterward which it was.

"Daddy, what's happening?" he asked, feeling remarkably calm for all the commotion.

"Go back to sleep, junior!" his dad told him, maybe a little more harshly than was necessary. Amazingly enough, the boy did just that.

His next memory was of waking while the family drove, calmly, to a nearby motel. His parents both seemed curiously silent, perhaps even a little sad, but never mentioned the strange incident on the road again. In time, the boy forgot about it completely, putting it out of his mind for many years. Although, he always retained a glimmer of a memory concerning an odd airplane that he had once seen while traveling the dusty highways out of Texas toward the Midwest. In time, this piece of his personal puzzle would begin to loom large in his mind.

The boy's father was soon transferred to Central America, Panama Canal district, during the eighties. It was at this time that the boy first began to realize that, perhaps, there was something more or less unusual about himself, and that he was not quite the average child. He began to spend endless hours alone, oftentimes daydreaming in his room, and his youthful love of reading was driven by a consuming interest in topic that most young people are, perhaps, better advised to not pursue. He devoured young adult books on ghosts, psychic powers, witchcraft, voodoo, even reincarnation and strange creatures. But his all-consuming passion was a study of books on UFOs, of which there were quite a selection available for young readers.

His mother, who had always indulged him his intellectual whims, was oblivious to his reading material, realizing that he had been raised on a steady diet of old science fiction and monster movies, and had always loved Halloween best of all holidays. His father, however, was less forgiving of his strange taste in reading material, and, coming home from work one day, and pawing through his son's collection of library books, suddenly stormed into the living room and demanded of his wife, "Why do you let him read that stuff? Ghosts, monsters, flying saucers? Witchcraft? Jesus, it's no wonder the kid can't sleep at night!"

The ensuing argument turned into quite a row, but the boy was permitted to retain his strange interests, as it seemed to be his chief comfort in the face of loneliness and boredom.

Of course, it was not merely young adult books on paranormal topics that kept the young boy awake at night. For nighttime was the time when the creeping feeling of unease generated by such books seemed to grow, intensify, and magnify until it resonated with a power that became real and palpable to a child lying huddled beneath the covers of his bed.

Once, upon awaking from a sound sleep, the boy was certain that he had seen his little dog enter the bedroom. He could clearly make out the animal in the streaming moonlight, as it sat, seemingly at attention, while the boy rubbed his eyes furiously free from sleep.

Perhaps it was a dream. At any rate, it could hardly be his pet, for that animal had died several weeks previously after being run over by a truck. The ghostly animal seemed to freeze in the moonlight, before fading into the gloom.

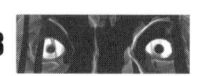

And that was not the only strange visitor to trouble the young boy's sleep. Another fleeting memory occurred to him years later, an image that seemed to be pulled from the recesses of a dream. Yet, considering the subsequent experiences of the boy (now a full-grown man), he finds it hard to discount the flashback so easily out of hand.

Lying in bed one dark night, the boy was astounded to see what looked like a little man with long arms, a little gnome-like creature from a fantasy story book, come ambling through the doorway into his room. It was difficult to see against the living room light (the boy always had to have the living room light on as he slept, lest he never sleep at all), but it was unmistakably a little, greenish, brown dwarf, and, what's more, it seemed to be carrying a sort of light, raised to the center of its chest. The light fell across the boy's forehead, and it was the last thing he remembered.

(It should be noted that, in Central America, where the boy was living at the time on a military base, reports of short, hairy UFO occupants were commonplace during the eighties, and form their own classification of UFO entity.)

Later, he dismissed this as yet another in a long series of befuddling dreams and vague half-memories. Of course, there were other incidents, experiences and encounters that happened while he was wide awake, that were far harder to dismiss as the residue of troubled dreaming.

The military housing addition where the boy lived was a number of multi-level white buildings, surrounding a wide courtyard where a few straggling playground pieces shard space with overhanging palm trees. Occasionally, one could sight a ring-tailed lizard or a particularly ferocious looking iguana scurry across the sidewalk and up a tree, but, on the whole, it was a pleasant enough place.

One day, as the boy was riding his bike around the courtyard, he passed an elderly black man, a black Panamanian who seemed strangely out of place for some reason. Of course, the boy dismissed him out of hand as a gardener or worker, but looking back upon the situation as it transpired, he is now not so sure. The boy pedaled past him, and approached an unoccupied dwelling, a house that looked as if it was closed up and had long been unoccupied.

Suddenly, he began to hear what he took, at first, to be the screech of a wild animal. He slowed his bicycle, stopping and balancing the bike on one leg as he stopped to listen. It was the sort of ferocious animal screech that one associated with the feral cats of the zoo, and he felt himself begin to be chilled. He scanned the trees above, but could see nothing there. The sound, as a matter of fact, seemed to be emerging from the vacant housing unit.

The windows he noted, were all closed. Yet, the strange sound had a stereophonic quality to it, as if it encompassed the place, clung to it, as much as emitted from it. It was, suddenly, a terrifying call of alert, but it was also fascinating, as it did not seem to emerge from anywhere that could be easily discerned. Instead, it increased in volume the closer one got to the house. The boy, despite his own fears, suddenly found himself putting the kickstand down, and approaching the house from the side, stepping up onto a small porch, toward a battered, locked back doorway.

The screeching growl grew more menacing. It was now encompassing all the sound that could be heard, enveloping the boy in its bizarre aural quality, striking fear into a heart that was already pumping quite fiercely. He could suddenly feel the cold chills of terror lick his skin, and something else: a sense of pervading evil, and gloom. It was a feeling that he was trespassing upon the territory of something that did not wish for him to be there. Then, as if in confirmation of his most spine-tingling fears, the cougar screech suddenly morphed, seeming to deepen and thicken with rage, until it was no longer the voice of an animal. Now, the boy was standing in the darkened porch way at the back of the house listening to the thunderous yell of an insane, invisible, human male. A male with the voice of a lion. A male that sounded as if he could rip the guts from a small boy in an insane act of pure, malicious vengeance. Yet this phantom screamer was nowhere in sight.

Suddenly, the boy found himself running, running from the icy clutches and the terrible phantom shrieks of that haunted building, forgetting all about the bike he had left parked out in front. He ran home on legs that felt like jelly, went to his room, and tried to still the hammering of his heart.

Immediately, his mother realized something was wrong. But, what could he tell her? There was nothing he could say about the incident which she would believe. Instead, he went cautiously back outside, telling her he had just gotten winded and need a short break from playing. Outside, on the back steps, he met his little friend, Scotty.

Not wanting to brave walking back to the house to get his bike, which was still parked, crookedly, on the sidewalk out front, he turned to his little friend, asking as innocently as possible, "Say, Scotty, my man. Would you go get my bike for me? I'll give you a dollar if you do."

The younger boy suddenly looked downcast and frightened.

"No," he shook his head sadly. "It scares me over there."

And that was all he would say. But it was enough to confirm for the boy that his strange experience was not something he had encountered alone.

He was never quite sure how he got his bike back, but he did. Of course, there were a few other experiences of note, most of them remembered only fleetingly, as if in flashback or the recall of a strange dream. One particularly vivid dream the boy experienced around this time had him awaking one night to be ushered out of his house by his parents and some other people he didn't know. He went out onto the streets of the military base, and saw his neighbors walking, in a massive group, toward the school sports field, as if they were eagerly expecting something. He followed along in the group, at times losing sight of his parents in the milling throng. It appeared to be the middle of the night.

Suddenly, as they came upon the baseball field, the masses of residents looked skyward, to see an enormous, orange, glowing craft come hovering forward above the trees. It was as if the entire community, guided by hypnotic forces they scarce understood, had been conditioned to come out and greet the visitors. But, of course, like so much else, he dismissed this as another dream.

Bedroom visitants, whether they were real or simply the product of hypnogogic dreams and sleep paralysis, also made themselves manifest from time to time. One thin, reed-like personage, with a large head and translucent skin, appeared in his room one morning as he was awaking from sleep. It was a thin, almost plant-like being with little stems for arms and legs, and a bulbous head, and it moved as if it were nearly weightless. The boy froze in bed, more amazed than frightened.

It seemed to dance, or even drift about on streams of air, before crumpling into an odd posture, and slowly disintegrating into the surrounding image of the dimly-lit bedroom. It was a creature from fantasy, sure enough. It was also not the most terrifying of visitants.

The most terrifying visitant the boy would encounter during these "sleep visitations" (or these encounters with what some might call the traditional "night hag") occurred first in Panama, Central America. One morning, the boy awoke to find that the dimensions of his room were, somehow, all wrong. The doorways and walls were tilting at crazy, non-Euclidean angles, and he wondered at the bizarre geometry that had suddenly seen fit to render the mundane aspects of his home something from a surrealist fever dream. It was then that he noticed the image looming in the doorway.

It was a monstrous thing with the outline of a giant bat; alternately, it was an enormous man in a black cloak that approximated bat wings, but whatever it was, it had no face. Simply a dark hood where a face should be, and an enormous shoulder-span and height that placed it well outside the range of anyone that could be construed as normally human.

Stunned—shocked into a terror so severe he literally felt his soul curl up inside himself, wither, and shrink to an animal state of panic—the boy felt himself torn between the bolt paralysis of being frozen in his bed, and the urge to get up and run from this monstrosity, this black demon, even jumping out the window if that is what it took. He started to scream for his mother, yet felt the words choke within his throat.

And just as suddenly, the thing seemed to turn with lightening speed, and shoot off ward into thin air. The boy felt the paralysis break, and as he jumped from bed he ran into the living room, realizing that his parents were still fast asleep. The contours of the walls and doorways and ceiling slowly began to right themselves again, but the fear was still strong. He would never, for the rest of his life, forget that feeling of all-consuming spiritual dread.

It was not long afterward that his father converted to fundamentalist Christianity, after telling an amazing story wherein Jesus had appeared to him one morning (really, literally appeared in the flesh), and chased him around the house before securing a promise of his forgiveness and subsequent salvation. Needless to say, with all of this going on in the boy's life, his early years were rife with strange, supernatural undercurrents, undercurrents that would only begin to make sense many years later, when he had finally grown into some sense of maturity.

As a teenager, the boy was plagued with depression and physical problems. It was at a stay in the hospital, while sleeping one night, that the boy was, once again, cursed with a visit by the monstrous black apparition that had tormented him several years before. It was the same being—an image of death. It was an enormous hooded figure with no face except for burning red eyes, and long skinny black fingers. It seemed to carry with it a cacophonous soundtrack of infernal moans. Its image was blacker than black, and it could be seen easily against the shadows of the night. The boy, who had at first assumed, after a night of miserable dreams, that he must have fallen asleep under a tree, realized that the branches that were threateningly close to touching his face were not tree branches, but the pointed, bony black fingers of the being that stood, immense, before him. By his bedside.

It was living evil. There was no goodness, no warmth, no humanity in that phantasmal form. It was death; it devoured souls and delighted in pain and torment. It was the opposite of God.

Beside this revenant, this image of death incarnate, was the proverbial Pale Horse. Or, at the very least, the bony, white body seemed to approximate that of a sickly mare. The emaciated thinness of the being beside the hooded one was as disturbing as any image from a concentration camp photo. It was bent, its body bearing some strange resemblance to that of a sleek, white greyhound, and every rib and bone was visible just beneath the skin. The arms, long and bony and punctuated by freakish bony fingers that were, likewise, of an abnormally long length, folded upward like those of a praying mantis, and, in truth, the thing could simply have been some mutant, outsized variation of that insect life form. The head was insectile as well: enormous black eyes, atop a huge cranium, and a chin that came down to a sharp point. There was no nose, and only a leering slit for a mouth. The thing moved in a strange, wobbly fashion, as if it was being pulled by the strings of a marionette.

Of course, these were phantoms, ghosts, not solid beings—and we don't mean to suggest that they were solid beings. The boy, having never been exposed to a sight so hideously repellent, felt himself paralyzed with terror. Suddenly, in what must have been an involuntary psychic break, he bolted forward in bed, seeming to see himself outside of himself, and screamed in sheer, maddened terror.

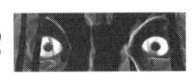

His last memories were of a hospital attendant bursting into his room, a flashlight in hand, and saying, "Oh, he must have been having some nightmare."

He sank down into merciful catatonia, having literally fainted in shock. The next day, his entire body felt terrible, and it took him several hours to remember that anything had even happened at all.

As he grew older, his interest in UFOs and the occult waxed and waned. He often spent long months thinking nothing of it, concentrating, as young people will, on rock music, or going to parties, or even school. Then, some faint remembrances and some vague feeling of inexplicable longing would steal over him, and he would begin to research the subject once more. He must have read fifty books on the subject in a few short years, oftentimes rereading the same stories over and over, and never failing interest.

One night, as he lay in bed in the throes of a strange dream, he imagined himself in a bright room. A short, squat little being with immensely long arms and greenish skin seemed to be ambling toward him, its outstretched embrace a nightmare of comical absurdity. The dreaming boy thought to himself, *"Is that freakin' ET?"* He laughed in his sleep.

Suddenly, he was awake, or, at the very least, he believed he was awake. His eyes fell upon a tall being clothed in shimmering white, with a great, bald head. The being seemed to be imperceptibly old, and its skin looked like wet clay. The eyes were enormous, ringed by wrinkled skin, but they were entirely normal. Or so it seemed.

It opened eyes that looked too small, altogether, for the head in which they were placed. The boy wondered, perhaps, if the thing was not wearing some sort of flesh-colored suit. He fell back into a strange darkness where a multitude of overlapping voices never seemed to quite make any sense, and in which he seemed to be spinning, madly, through a chasm from which he could never hope to reach bottom.

Many years later he was married, but the strange, occasional obsession with UFOs would continue. He and his wife would, upon occasion, spot many small, glowing lights in the sky, and wonder. One night, after spending an absurd evening looking out a fourth-story window at passers in the street below, they were astounded to see a bright, glowing star-like object suddenly spark up over a nearby sports field. It went slowly, silently, behind the building in which they lived, before reappearing suddenly on the other side. And disappearing again.

And that was not all. There was the ride back from visiting the in-laws, when a detour through the Indiana countryside became a disorienting excursion into unfamiliar territory. His wife, who had been driving, found herself becoming quite lost, although she had known the way before.

Hours later, they arrived home. Yet, when looking at the clock on the mantle, they realized they were actually far later in getting home then they should have been. What happened to a missing hour or more, neither of them could say.

The reader may now be asking themselves what, exactly, to make of all of this. The theory that certain humans, for whatever reasons, are gifted (or, alternately, cursed) to have encounters with unknown beings is a facet of the human experience as old as the mythological lore of gods, fairies, sylphs, brownies, and leprechauns. Our modern variation appears to be a strange, transient phenomenon of individuals who, at certain times, are confronted or abducted by beings that science can not rationally explain. But is it all in their minds?

Budd Hopkins, a long-time researcher in the field of "UFO abductions" doesn't think so. According to his theory, which he has outlined in bestselling books like *Intruders* and *Missing Time*, the phenomenon is quite real, clandestine, and the result of a long-range "breeding" or "eugenics" program carried on by our extraterrestrial counterparts in the hopes of, quite possibly, replenishing the stock of their own DNA. Popular author Whitley Strieber's bestselling book *Communion* covers much the same territory, although he withholds judgment, seemingly, on who the visitors actually are and where they originate from, and why. Strieber documents his own experience from the eighties when, while vacationing at a cabin in upstate New York, he awoke one evening to find a little blue man with a curious black circle for a mouth approaching his bedside.

What followed was a painful and humiliating examination aboard an apparent UFO vehicle. Then a sort of amnesiac screening was placed upon him, which could only be broken through with the help of a controversial technique referred to as *regressive hypnosis*, wherein an often self-appointed "specialist" will hypnotize a patient in the hopes of helping the subject recall memories that are too frightening or bizarre for the waking mind to cope with.

This technique has been the subject of much heated speculation concerning the final, objective value of any information gained thereby (as some naysayer make the accusation that subjects can easily be "led" to give whatever sort of fantastical and spurious information the hypnotist wants), but I digress.

Many times, such "abductees," (or, alternately, "experiencers" as they sometimes like to be referred to), are made to give blood or semen samples, or, in the case of females, are reported to have eggs removed. These individuals then report that frail, gray-skinned "extraterrestrials" often show them about the ship, including taking them to laboratories where hybrid "children" (the result of alien/human cross-fertilization) float in test-tubes. On rare occasions, experiencers are shown hybrid "children," or made to hold a hybrid baby.

It's obviously unsettling stuff.

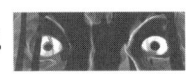

Of course, there are those that believe that such events exist only in the minds of overly-imaginative people. Some researchers, such as folklorist Thomas Bullard and computer scientist Jacques Vallee, have drawn parallels between the ancient accounts of witches Sabbaths, incubi, elves, abduction to "fairyland," and other bizarre, anomalous tales of the distant past to try and assert a pattern of extraordinary human experience that suggests…something. Vallee posits that our Extra-normal visitors, rather than being visitors from some strange planet, may in fact be the denizens of an entirely unplumbed dimension, or level of reality as foreign to us as anything we can imagine. His book *Dimensions* is itself a breathtaking nightmare ride through the weird and wonderful landscape inhabited by Marian apparitions, aerial swimmers, and alien elves bearing crispy pancakes. All adventurous souls are advised to seek out this worthy volume.

Mr. Vallee has likewise postulated in his book *Messengers of Deception* that the entire phenomenon may be staged, perhaps by an international cult (the Raelians come to mind) or a secret government body in preparation for bringing about fascism or some sort of mass system of population control. He speculates they could do this through the use of propaganda techniques, hypnosis, and perhaps even holographic images and agents dressed in alien garb.

Curiously, an Internet legend, a supposed secret "Project Blue Beam," has long circulated the cyber highways, giving testimony to a supposed plan by the CIA to either:

A: use high-intensity holographic projection technology to create an illusion of the second coming of Christ, or

B: do the same thing to fake a full-scale alien invasion.

As to what purpose the CIA (or whatever nefarious, mysterious agency would be behind such an outstandingly bizarre performance), could have for staging such an event, can only be for us a matter of speculation and conjecture.

An altogether more reasonable (as far as THIS writer is concerned) hypothesis concerning the UFO enigma comes to us from none other than John Alva Keel, the author of *The Mothman Prophecies*, a book thats central enigma, a mysterious eight-foot creature with no head, red glowing eyes, and great moth-like wings, actually takes a backseat to even stranger goings on in the small town of Point Pleasant, West Virginia, in 1966.

Keel, who personally investigated the mysterious sightings of "Mothman," the reported UFO encounters of contactee Woodrow Durenberger (who was approached by a bizarre emissary of the netherworld who went by the moniker of "Indrid Cold"), and who reported chasing blue UFOs hovering across a field, is a man who certainly seems to know the terrain he seemed destined to chronicle. Keel, during the space of his investigation, began to receive menacing phone calls from "Mr. Cold" himself, was followed by mysterious black Cadillacs, was haunted by the image of MIB ("Men in Black," a common enough UFO phantasm that some credit as being pale-skinned, black-suited government agents, others as extraterrestrials in disguise), and claimed he more than once awoke with an enormous black image standing over him, leaving him frozen in terror.

His phone, which becomes a central part of the paranormal activity outlined in the book, begins to receive strange chatter, and of course, calls from the mysterious psychic entity "Indrid Cold." Mr. Keel describes going to some length to trace down whatever could be the matter with the telephones he was using. (One particularly troubling incident involved a nonsensical voice that would call from out of the blue, and proceed to speak at an alarming and high-pitched rate that was quite beyond comprehension. Curiously, the boy who we've been discussing in this chapter also had a similar phenomenon happen to him at one point.)

It was all to no avail. Mr. Keel continued to experience the strange presence of "Indrid Cold" and the bizarre happenings that overshadowed and haunted his life right up until the collapse of the Silver Bridge over the Ohio River, on December 15th, 1967. According to Wikipedia, an online resource, the "bridge was loaded with rush-hour traffic." Forty-six people were killed.

Mr. Keel claims in his book that Indrid Cold as much prophesied the collapse, as well as other events which didn't, strangely enough, transpire. Keel went on to write the book *UFOs: Operation Trojan Horse*, an exhaustive study of the phenomenon that traces UFOs through Biblical allusions, mythology, Scandinavian "ghost rockets," "Deros," "Foo Fighters" (Strange aerial objects sighted by WW2 combat pilots—they were at first assumed to be secret Nazi technology, until it was discovered, after the war, that the Nazis reported them, too!), and the modern contacts and abductions of people like George Adamski, Truman Bethurum, and the much more believable experience of Betty and Barney Hill.

His final conclusion? UFOs represented a sometimes malignant, but possibly amoral energy force somewhere in the lower, or infrared frequency band, that was both incalculably old and beyond the mind's ability at comprehension. Perhaps God, to us; most definitely a sort of entity that defies the mind's ability at rational absorption.

This force is, by and large, responsible for the myriads of inexplicable supernatural occurrences that have plagued mankind since the dawn of time, including: bizarre religious phenomenon, manifestations of ghosts, gods, and spirits, strange prophecies (it can see, apparently, around the bend of our present space-time continuum) and many other odd, inexplicable, and incongruent occurrences that act, as Keel explains, in the capacity of a "Trojan Horse," allowing this monstrous (to our way of thinking) entity a sort of primitive attempt at communication with its inferiors. Of course, the fact that such an awesome and inconceivable mind might find it a tricky business to communicate with such a finite species of sentient life as mankind, might necessitate some bizarre, and unearthly means of getting the local inhabitants' attention. Alternately, the very modes of thought by which such a fantastical, god-like being operate might be so inconceivable to our tiny, miniscule grasp of consciousness, that we may have simply been misunderstanding the various phenomena low these many centuries. Keel postulates that the various manifestations of UFO craft and their pilots are little more than temporary anomalies, mannequins or marionettes, designed to convey the physical manifestation of something that cannot exist within the parameters of our finite comprehension.

Hence, strange, incongruent tales of UFO creatures of all variant shapes, sizes, and colors, as well as stories of "flying saucers" that seem to be comprised of little more than hammered together junk, with bits and pieces of them continuously falling off.

As a strange side note, Keel suggests that this creation of "temporary anomalies" or "Trojan horses" might account for the mysterious mutilation of cattle, who are often found, after heavy UFO activity, to be lying in otherwise inaccessible fields, exsanguinated and seemingly surgically dissected. Could it be that this overweening "Overlord of the UFO" needs the biological material and blood plasma of cattle and other critters to form extraterrestrial "robots," or biomechanical freaks to fly around in brilliant ships that are nothing more than collections of ordinary junk? Are we perhaps going off the rails a bit?

John Keel also uses the analogy of a student staring into a Petri dish through a powerful microscope, looking on in wonder at the myriad life forms represented in the primordial soup below. Each life form will have a microscopic lifespan, comparatively, to the student who is busily observing them, and the life forms themselves will be no more cognizant of the fact that they are being watched than we would be if a much greater, infinitely older intelligence were busily observing us (and many billions reckon one probably is).

Of course, this hypothesis could be used to explain the various stories of UFO crashes as well, stories that are replete with tales of miniscule bodies with few (if any) internal organs, and "spacecraft" that seem to have been fitted together from tinfoil and balsawood. Who can say?

One thing is for certain though, the boy, and millions of others like him, have continued, throughout their lives, to harbor half-memories and strange flashbacks of incidents involving mysterious flying objects and their occupants. We can only speculate and attempt to reconstruct from those vague memories and half-remembered suppositions what might have happened during those critical "missing hours."

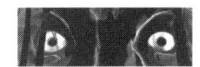

The boy and his aunt were walking down the sidewalk, minding their own business, enraptured a little by the warmth of the night, the wide expanse of stars above them, and the relative warmth of their friendship.

They hadn't a care in the world, nor any thought of danger, until the black van pulled up beside them.

They hadn't heard this particular vehicle, had most likely not been paying any attention, and later couldn't even remember if it had been driving with the headlights on or off.

"Hey, you guys want to go for a ride?"

The boy and his aunt exchanged nervous glances, stopping, foolishly enough, almost in mid-stride. The van was idling, now, in the middle of the street.

A strange, pale face was thrust out the window. A thin face with black hair, and dark eyes. Later, they would each be able to remember nothing out of the ordinary about the man, nor anything else about him particularly striking, for that matter. He seemed to be a fairly young chap, with his hair parted to the side, and he seemed to be a little too anxious to have them accompany him along for the ride.

Suddenly, the boy's aunt did something unexpected. She seemed to shake her head a little, as if coming to some sort of recognition, and then approached the man where he leaned out of the passenger side window.

"Oh, oh it's you! Jesus, man, you scared the hell out of me!"

The boy was uncertain of what was going on, but he thought, perhaps this was someone his aunt knew, and so he followed her to the passenger side window, putting his hands on his hips importantly and trying to catch his breath from so much walking.

"Long time no see, huh?"

"Sure," replied the boy's aunt. "I guess it has been awhile."

The boy tried to get a good look at the man's face, but the shadows seemed to prevent it, and besides, he was obviously some acquaintance of his aunt's. Possibly an old boyfriend. And didn't he look just a little bit familiar, after all?

"So what are you guys doing, huh? Out to see the stars?"

"Oh, just walking for exercise. Oh, this is my nephew, by the way."

"I know."

I know, the man in the van had said. But the boy wondered how, exactly, he knew. After all, the boy had no particularly memory of this man, and couldn't seem to even get a very good look of him in the strange, purple light that seemed to be emanating from the interior of the vehicle. He couldn't see the driver, but whoever it was, he seemed to be sitting, stock still, staring ahead at the winding road through the neighborhood.

"Sure we can't give you guys a lift?"

His aunt, whose voice seemed to have slowed a little, taking on a confused, almost dreamy state, replied, amazingly enough, "Sure."

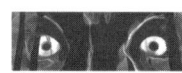

Before the boy knew it, he was seated beside her in the back of the van.

"No need to strap yourselves in," said the man. "We're not going to be going very far."

The entire incident now took on the bizarre aspects of some disconnected dream. The boy turned to his aunt, said, "Are you sure this was a good idea?"

"No," she said, matter-of-factly. "I'm not sure why we're here."

"You're here," said the stranger in the passenger seat, who now inexplicably seemed much older, paler, and whose face now seemed to be waxen and stiff, "because we've invited you. You're a very lucky pair of people to get to see what you're going to see tonight."

"I want to leave."   The boy felt panic grip his insides.

His aunt finally seemed to snap back to a vague sort of reality, and said, "Hey, why don't you guys just let us out here, okay? We'll be alright. We can walk home."

He felt her grip his arm, whisper to him, "Shoo, it will be okay. Don't panic."

The man laughed, not a sound the boy would ever relish hearing again (it had a dry, mechanical, rasping sound to it that was quite unnerving), and suddenly he realized that the man sitting in the passenger seat had transformed himself almost entirely. He was now no longer a faintly handsome young man of rough-hewn features. Now he seemed very old: The side of his face that was visible as he turned was old, wrinkled, waxen white. Amazingly, now he was wearing a hat, a dark fedora. Also, for some reason, he was now wearing dark sunglasses, although the interior of the van was quite darkly purple.

"You won't be harmed. There's nothing to fear from us."

"You guys don't have the right to do this to people," his aunt said lamely.

"We have a right."

"Who are you guys?" asked the boy.

The man, who had settled back in the passenger seat, suddenly seemed to think better of it. As if to answer the boy's question, he leaned forward, half-turning to the duo in the back seat, and with one gnarled, skinny hand, removed the black shades from his eyes.

The resultant shock was almost a delayed reaction, but both the boy and his aunt began to scream. There was something wrong with the man's eyes. No human being should have eyes like that. It was beyond deformity; it was monstrous.

Just as suddenly as they had erupted into tears of shock and fright, a strange calm seemed to steal over them, and the subsequent events took on the disconnected aspects of a strange, disembodied dream. The boy (and most likely his aunt, too) seemed to be standing outside of himself watching events unfold. Suddenly, he was certain he was having a nightmare. The man in the passenger seat turned back toward the windshield and said nothing

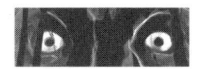

more. The driver was stock-still as he operated the vehicle, and never turned toward them at all.

The next thing they knew they were standing in the enormous field across the street from the aunt's apartment complex. The van was parked beside them, but soon disappeared. They had not even heard it drive away, and never saw it again.

They waited, but it was not long before they realized what they had been brought here for. Above them, suddenly, a brilliant ring of lights seemed to burst forth in the darkened sky. They encircled a dark, menacing craft, which seemed enormous as it hovered, silently, above them. The boy now knew he was dreaming, but involuntarily reached out to grab his aunt's hand for a sense of security. They continued to stare upward at the brilliantly-lit dark object, when, suddenly, a bright blue beam emanated down from the center of the craft, encircling them in tingling, electrostatic charge. The force of this particular beam seemed incredible.

It was a moment before they found themselves surrounded by a trio of strange, skinny, little men with large heads, and enormous black eyes. Their arms and legs were thin to the point of emaciation, and they seemed to not be wearing clothing, yet nothing definite could be ascertained about their anatomy. Their fingers were long, crooked claws, but they seemed to be gentle, and they had straight slits for mouths. The noses were ill-defined; mere holes on a bump in the face. The chins went down to sharp points.

Their lips never moved, but amazingly, they seemed to speak directly to the boy's mind.

Come with us. Don't be afraid. We aren't going to hurt you.

"Where are you taking us?" asked the boy's aunt.

We're just going to give you a little examination. You won't be hurt, and you may learn something that most of your own people aren't lucky enough to ever know. Now come.

"You don't have a right to do this to people."

We have a right. Don't be afraid. You won't be harmed.

Suddenly, they were surrounded by the small beings, and felt themselves floating upward, as if in the thralls of a lucid dream, bathed in the powerful force of the mysterious light. By some means of which they never ascertained, they had entered the alien craft.

The next thing they encountered was being led through a series of bright, evenly-lit corridors. The boy suddenly realized that he had been separated from his aunt, but he was too astounded to even protest or worry. He was led by one of the strange little occupants into a perfectly round room, also evenly-lighted, with a sort of combination chair and operating table. A mind geared to understanding engineering would have noted the fact that the interior of

the UFO seemed to have been "injection molded"—everything was perfectly sculpted into the floor and walls. There was nary a hint, though, of any sort of mechanism or controls.

The boy, who felt a curious mixture of shock and disassociation, was laid upon the table by one of the small gray beings. It was not uncomfortable, but he felt the fear began to creep back into his mind, as the strange hypnosis began to inexplicably wane. The strange abductors who had taken him and his aunt were so ugly, their eyes being the worst—truly grotesque, amazing and black, and seemingly fathomless. They were like the eyes of monstrous insects, and the boy began to shudder in the coolness of the examining room interior. He realized that he was momentarily alone.

He couldn't move. He seemed to be suffering utter paralysis, and even though there were no bands holding down his arms, he found himself unable to even budge them. He found himself blacking out intermittently, perhaps from fear.

He snapped his eyes open and found himself staring into the hideous visage of one of the beings. His great black eyes stared into the boy's own, seemingly looking down into his very soul, and the boy suddenly realized that one of the long, skinny hands held a strange, thin, needle-like instrument, with a little ball on the end of it. He thrust it forward.

"No! Please!"

The boy felt himself jerk involuntarily, but the rod was thrust into his eye, or rather behind it. The pain and discomfort seemed intense, but a long stroke of the alien's gray, skinny finger quieted the fear and nullified the trauma.

"What was that?"

I can't tell you that. But take heart. We're almost finished here.

Several other beings entered. Some of them seemed to be subordinates, or workers. One of them scraped something over his skin, but it was not painful. Another seemed to use a tube to draw blood.

The most frightening moment was the strange machine that seemed to descend from the ceiling (the boy hadn't noticed it before), and began to move across his body like an enormous electronic eye. It was apparently robotic, but it blinded him with a blast of violet light, and it moved as weirdly, as snake-like as if itself was a living thing. It then returned to its original position somewhere above, and the examination seemed to be complete.

One of the beings led him from the examining room down a darker corridor, speaking to him reassuringly as he went.

Now see, that wasn't so very bad, was it? Everything is going to be just fine. Why, when you're finished here, you'll be safe and sound again at home, and you'll begin to forget.

"But, who are you? And where do you come from? Why are you doing this?"

We have our own reasons. Most of which, you wouldn't understand. But I'm going to show you some things, some things that you may find to be very frightening, at first. But don't worry, we're only going to show you what might happen if the people of your world don't change their ways. It doesn't have to be the way we predict.

The boy next found himself standing in what appeared, for all the world, to be a miniature screening-room, or theatre. He was sat in front of a screen, and saw a series of images begin to move past very quickly.

The images were terrifying. They were movies of war, devastation, riots, terrorism, famine, and ecological disaster on a scale never before imagined. Rapidly, the boy saw burning cities, emaciated people in destitute villages, tanks and soldiers firing at each other and bulldozing homes, and columns of prisoners being marched to execution. There were tidal waves, earthquakes leveling cities, explosions, and hospital corridors in foreign lands, filled to overflowing with plague-pocked people who seemed barely alive.

Volcanoes erupted, tsunamis beat coastlines eradicating thousands, high towers came crashing down, and television anchors gave reports of widespread depression and economic catastrophe as images of starving people filled soup-lines and cities descended into scenes of violent squalor. Suddenly, the screened filled with visions of suited men, all arguing like children under the banner of various flags: American, German, British, French, Arabian. Iranian, Russian, Chinese, Israeli, and so forth. Missiles pierced the skies in many places, followed by terrific nuclear explosions, mushroom clouds boiling into the turbulent heavens as darkness descended upon a burned out world.

Your planet is in trouble. The water is poisoned, and the air is toxic. The world is waking up to your abuse, and your species is on the verge of destroying itself and all other life on Earth. What a strange, self-destructive species you are.

Suddenly, the screen darkened to the image of a burned-out cinder of a world, and disappeared altogether. The boy found himself standing with another being, a much taller being, beside him. This being was wearing a strange, dark cloak, with a hood, and seemed much more menacing, or frightening, than the little gray creatures the boy had been introduced to so far. He pointed toward the screen with one long, bony black finger, and it disappeared completely. Beyond, in the darkness, there seemed to be a sort of raised dais. Suddenly, a weird grayish illuminating pool of light seemed to flow down from the ceiling of the craft.

On the dais, a hideous thing of incalculable age, a creature more fantastic and repulsive than any the boy had yet encountered, stood hunkered over what appeared to be a control panel. Unlike the other beings he had been surrounded by since he had been brought aboard, this particular being had no pretensions to being even remotely related to human.

It was thoroughly insect-like, a hunched, gray, demonic figure with an enormous cranium, an arched, bony back, and immensely long arms that folded, praying mantis-like, in front of it. The fingers were long and skeletal,

as well as the legs. The thighbones could be clearly delineated, and the neck was a thin bony reed. The head, skull-like, was truly prodigious, and the mouth was a brutal slit.

But it was the eyes, the magnificent, black, teardrop-shaped eyes that wrapped around the white skull of the being, that put the rest of the image to shame. They were far larger than the eyes of the other beings, enormous, obsidian jewels that emitted evil. The thing moved in a strange, jerky fashion, and its long, bony frame seemed to be part horse, part praying mantis.

In short, it was a gigantic, mutant bug. And a fiercely intelligent and malignant one, at that. The boy felt terror grip his heart, and the thing shot a glance at him that seemed to have all the cold calculation of all the hate in the world projecting from the black depths of its reflective orbs. He could see himself in those eyes, and could feel the alien glance surmise and calculate and catalog and consider his weaknesses in one hellish appraisal.

Was this then the controller of the ship? The "captain" of the others. Was this then the "Leader?"

The boy would never know, for the next moment of consciousness he experienced was of being led down another curving corridor, this one more brightly lit than the one leading to the screening room. (Or control room, perhaps?) It was very cold all of a sudden, and the being beside him was now one of the regular grays, a being who seemed kind, if ugly, and consoling, if controlling.

The boy was led through a sliding doorway into a room that was deeply bright and cold. It seemed to be some sort of laboratory. Lining the walls were a number of glass tubes or jars. The being led the boy forward, and pointed to one of the jars lining the wall.

Inside, a curled blob, an apparent fetus, was preserved in a clear liquid.

"What is that? What are you doing with these…babies?"

The fetus looked malformed. The boy was reminded of the "pickled punk" exhibits he had once read about in a book about old-time carnivals.

They're alive. They're the future.

"I don't understand."

The being didn't explain, but suddenly, the door of the laboratory slid open, and his aunt, who he had completely forgotten during the entire strange ordeal, stepped through, accompanied by one of the grays, and another, small-ish being in a white smock.

The boy realized that she was naked, and that he was as well. However, he felt no shame. The being with his aunt seemed friendly, even apologetic, and pointed toward his aunt, and then toward the little being in the smock that stood beside her. The little being in the white smock grabbed his aunt's hand, and said, vocally, "My name is Lyrra."

The little being was some sort of hybrid, a cross between human and alien. It had wispy, white hair, thin and straggling, and huge eyes above a pointed chin and small mouth. But the eyes were normal, not solid black.

There will be many more of us coming. Many of us are already living among you. The time is growing late, and the clocks are ticking. The planet upon which you live is going to undergo great changes in the coming years, and many will not survive. Those that do will enter a new era of wonder and possibility. Until then, remember: We are watching, always.

It was then that the lights faded out on the entire experience, and the boy and his aunt found themselves walking down the sidewalk across the street from the apartment complex.

Suddenly, the aunt looked off at something that was coming up over the field across the street.

"Hey, what's that?"

The boy, who had been talking rather aimlessly about starting high school, and what rock bands he liked, and what girls were most popular, looked off in the distance, and said "It's a helicopter."

"Uh, it's not making any noise."

Sure enough, the great black object rose silently above the field, lit on each end by brilliant red lights, and giving off an occasional streak of lightening-like power from the top of it as it ascended, at a bizarre angle, to a hovering point above the heads of the startled witnesses. Whatever it was, it was silent, and it was huge.

It seemed to slow for a moment, perhaps building up momentum or speed, before exploding in a dark red cloud of light, and whisking away in a gravity-defying hop that was less flying than teleporting. It was the swiftest motion of an aerial object that either of them had ever seen. It was probably one of the most fantastic aerial feat that had ever been witnessed by human beings since the beginning of time.

It faded to a bright red star in the distance, before disappearing completely. The boy and his aunt felt themselves frozen for a moment, before the aunt said, "What in the hell was that?"

"That…was somebody that's just a little off course. By about six million light years!"

The boy began to laugh loudly, but they both suddenly felt afraid, and walked back to the apartment, slowly. As soon as they entered, the boy's mother demanded where the two of them had been and what had taken them so long. Neither of them could answer beyond a sort of vague recollection of having had a "close encounter" with something very unusual, something that couldn't be easily explained away. But neither of them could say much more than that, or remember anything else beyond the bits and pieces that would float up from their subconscious minds in dreams and at odd intervals. And that, for all intents and purposes, brings us back to where we first began.

27

The Hand and the Eye

T he boy continued to have, intermittently, strange experiences for many years. In college, while undergoing an intense depression, he began to experience the strange obsession with UFOs and alien life forms that seemed to surface in his mind intermittently.

During a bitter depression, when he was sick and tired of life, and looking for an answer to all the perplexing mysteries and conundrums that had presented themselves to him during his short time on this earth, he began to experience strange incidents, once again.

There were perplexing visions of bodies floating, in massive numbers, into the air. Although he didn't quite know how to interpret this, he wondered if perhaps in the future, some startling invention might replace automobiles and allow men to fly, unencumbered by the constraints of gravity. His brain was often aflame with such strange ideas; he sometimes felt as if he were being invaded.

He was bitterly depressed, though. A long-term relationship he had been involved in had ended abruptly and badly, and he felt himself quite lonely and uncared for. This began to be reflected in his personal habits; his dress became sloppy, his hygiene was lacking.

He walked the streets in a kind of somnambulistic daze at times; many people thought him to be crazy, and perhaps he was. Perhaps, in truth, we all are, and that is the only way to survive in a world that is so often, fundamentally, upside down.

He had always been taught, since the time he was a child, that God was somewhere off in heaven, watching over all of his children with a benevolent, caring eye. The ways of God might well be inscrutable at times, certainly would always remain a mystery to the common man or layperson, but they were not, he had been warned, specifically to be questioned. Yet, at this point in his life, he felt he could do little otherwise.

He quickly lost interest in college studies, sliding by as easily as he could with as little effort as possible. He virtually quit speaking to everyone around him, and the night, and his incessant walks at night, became his only friend.

At the same time, he began to sense, in his inner world, a strange, even alien force take possession of him. It was a cold, relentless entity,

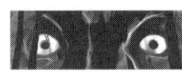

another personality that was detached, impersonal, and committed to an action or work the boy himself could not fully understand. Whatever it was, he began to doubt his own sanity, and in the space of several months of this idle, aimless, unmotivated existence, he began to think of doing himself in.

Of course, the suicide is, by dint of our own personal religious prejudices, considered to be the most unforgivable of all deaths. No matter how painful life is, we seem to assume, it is far better to sully up under the weight of an agonizing emotional or physical torment, than to take the plunge into death, that "undiscovered country, from whence once borne no traveler ever returns."

(We believe we've quoted that right, but we can't be positive just now.)

The suicide is the stuff from which ghostly legends and searing stories of hellfire and damnation are drawn. Suicides are assumed to lurk, in somber remembrance of their grievous mistake, as forlorn phantoms of the hereafter, shuffling through dim corridors and tapping on walls, or violently pulling the covers off of old beds before rapping loudly on the headboard. We can't swear for the veracity of any of these claims, but we have heard them whispered a time or two.

Alternately, those who have clinically died and claimed a "return" from the lands beyond, have noted that, as they were attempted suicides, no flowing angels of mercy or beings of light came forth from heavenly tunnels to greet them on their way toward perpetual bliss. Instead, they relate shuddering, terrifying tales of eternal darkness, weeping, wailing and gnashing of teeth, reptilian monsters (not at all an uncommon entity in the annals of paranormal lore) and even the occasional whiff of brimstone and flicker of hellfire.

Our boy, cognizant of all of this, perhaps even more so than the average individual (who tries with all his will to avoid placing an overemphasis of thought upon the final residence of his mortal spirit or consciousness) thankfully did not commit suicide. Although he tried, but that is another tale, for another time.

One day, in the late afternoon, after picking up a Bible and finding scant comfort within its mostly inscrutable pages, he violently closed the leather-bound cover, and slammed his fist into it. Repeatedly. Heatedly. He wanted answers, and none had seemed to be forthcoming for many, many months now.

He lay down upon his bed. He closed his eyes, yet, he felt no exhaustion, and knew he wasn't asleep. Instead, he found himself…transported. Delivered. Taken to a new and frightening place and shown strange things he had never before witnessed in his entire life.

It was a dark, primordial world, a place as barren and rough as the landscape of the lunar surface. But it was, unmistakably, Earth, and upon the surface of the planet the boy saw a vision of primitive man, not quite Neanderthal, but much more fully evolved. Shaggy, clad in furs, carrying rough spears and clubs, they roughly approximated the image one might have of African natives or Kalahari Bushmen. Yet, instead of a steaming jungle, their world seemed to be a vast, ugly, rocky desert with little in the way of vegetation and water.

And obviously, they were divided into hostile tribes.

Much went on like this in the vision, starting and stopping, showing flashes of scenes that faded into days and finally weeks and maybe years, until, soon, the vision began to shift. A group of the primitives had gathered around a fire in the chill early evening, when, suddenly, the leader, perhaps the tribal chieftain, stood up and leaned against his spear. Above him, a brilliant star began to glow brighter and brighter in the heavens. Soon, he called the attention of the rest of his people.

The glowing object grew to an enormous size, and suddenly, to the amazement of the primitive people gathered below, they could see that it was no ordinary comet or other such naturally-occurring aerial object. It was something entirely different from anything they had been exposed to in their entire lives.

It presented itself as a perfect black cube, brilliantly lit with shifting lights, and made from a solid material none of them had ever before had the experience of encountering. The surface was as dark as midnight.

It hovered, miraculously, just above their heads, before settling down into the midst of them, but never quite touching the ground.

The people, who had a rough language of grunts and clicks, began to speak madly amongst themselves, and even the mighty chieftain

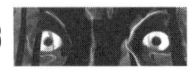

felt his bold, sturdy legs quiver with fear, as he pointed his spear at it, menacingly.

Suddenly, from the surface of the object, a multiplicity of strange sounds began to erupt, voices, speaking in a number of strange tongues that the people couldn't possibly have known. They began to grunt and click amongst themselves again, and the cube from space suddenly ceased its bizarre chatter, and began to make noises as if it was calculating and assimilating the unwritten language of the primitives.

In a short time, it was communicating with them effectively.

Of course, there was no doubt in the minds of the tribesmen that this was God, or a god, or at the very least a personage worthy of veneration and worship. First and foremost, however, the Cube from Space acted as a Great Teacher. And what lessons those primitives soon learned.

From hunter-gatherers to more effective hunters, and from there to planting and irrigation. From primitive, superstitious witch doctoring to mastering a few basic arts of medicine and survival; from spears to clumsy stone axes, and later to blunt instruments that were rudimentary swords.

The dwellings went from being thatched huts that blew away miserably in a violent storm of dust, to sturdy clay buildings that could house and shelter a family—and families did soon grow. And systems grew from the need for order, and religion grew to chastise the people when they misbehaved, and Law grew from the necessity to punish the wrongdoers.

A religion was born around the mastery of the Cube, and the Cube did little to protest this itself. After all, it guided evolution along a trajectory that had been programmed for it by one greater than it, and its understanding of the finer points of ethical direction might have been somewhat lacking. Soon, the Cube found itself put upon a pedestal, offered sacrifices of goats and other livestock (domestication had proceeded at an acceptable, even admirable rate) and its increasingly refined musings were taken by the people as holy writ. And yes, soon, they were even plunking down chicken-scratches in crude stone tablets, and a history was about to be born.

All of this was good, saw the Cube, who felt as if it could rest a bit on its laurels, and could foresee no real reason to worry about the immediate future, as things were proceeding nicely.

Of course, the success of one tribe, inevitably, brought the envy of others, who watched the strange goings-on below them from their perches and aeries in the vast hills and rocky mountains surrounding the now fertile valley below. A contemptuous mixture of envy and fear began to eat at these out-dwelling primitives, and they soon wondered why their own gods had, as of late, been so dismissive of them. After all, they were just barely subsisting on what they could gather, and the pickings as far as animal flesh were slim. Their women did not possess the lustrous comeliness of the better-fed brides below, nor were their own dwellings as sturdy and impregnable as the dwellings of the rival tribe that lived in a valley that had been transformed, in such a short time, into a place lush and wondrous and green.

And of course, they wondered at the strange black stone, the one that looked to be perfectly formed on all sides, with nary a ripple or debasement on its smooth, obsidian surface. They also wondered at the melodious, patient voice that came forth from this "magic boulder," and they thought, perhaps, the whole thing was possessed full of monsters or spirits.

Their own god, a badly chiseled hunk of rock that remained silent, and useless, and aloof, had not blessed them the way that this other god had blessed their neighbors in the valley, and their chieftain began to wonder why. Were they not as worthy as the people below? Had they not served their god, and offered sacrifices to him at each phase of the moon? Were they simply bad, or incorrigible in some way, or less attractive? Were their daughters not comely, too?

The chieftain of the mountain tribe was having none of it, and one day, much to the horror of the tribal elders, he approached the altar of their silent, mocking, useless god, and he pushed the graven image from its pedestal, shattering it upon the rough earth. One man fell dead away in shock, and others declared that he had just cursed himself and his descendants to the fortieth generation, but it was really no great episode, after awhile. Most of the tribe had been tired of serving that particular god, anyway, seeing as how he had never in his long history been very kind, generous, or forgiving. No, the god below them, the black god of their enemy tribe (whom they had made war with before, and had always managed to at least best, if not totally eradicate), was a much more propitious fellow altogether, it seemed, and serving him, undoubtedly, was the thing to do, for the good of all.

However, how could they go about getting rid of his chosen children, the hated tribe of the Lower Valley that he seemed to now be so favoring with rich knowledge and miraculous rewards? That was a problem that was going to need some consulting upon, and so the

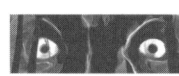

chieftain called a council of his elders together, and included among them one known, generally, as seer of spirits and far-off worlds where gods and immortal beings walked together with the dead.

This particular shaman, who was clad in a cloak of black feathers and who had a long, pale face, no teeth, and a pair of burning, haunted eyes, looked deep within the smoke from the ceremonial fire where, he claimed, he could see the dancing vision of the future in the leaping tongues of flame. It was one of war, he claimed: A black spirit, the Spirit of the Ages, had told him that they must prepare to do battle with the people below, and then they would find favor with the strange god that had come from the sky, as he would then deem them worthy to be His children, and would favor them and curse his former charges as weaklings and cowards.

Of course, the chieftain and the elders knew that such an all-out offensive was not going to be an easy task. For one, the people in the valley below were better fed, better prepared and sheltered, and had fashioned for themselves superior weaponry that was going to be difficult to match with clumsy spears and ignorant clubs.

No matter, said the Old Wise Seer. It was how the spirits said it must be, and so thus it must transpire. They should prepare, he said, with hundreds of men and women, recruited from the caves and cul-de-sacs of the hillsides and mountain ranges, and arm them with spears, and most importantly, torches. For, they would burn the crops in the fertile valley, and kill they domesticated beasts, and lay waste to the infant farmland that had sprung up in the shadow of the Cube.

And so it was they began to prepare for the First Great War mankind would ever know.

The Cube itself was not completely ignorant of the preceding events, since it monitored activity around it with super-sensitive accuracy and realized that something was brewing in the primitive lands just above. It was a few days of panic when the people, emerging from their stone huts one day, found that the Great Throne of the Cube was vacant, and that their god had, seemingly, vanished without a trace. There was wailing and gnashing of teeth, and quite a lot of blood flowed from sacrificed animals, in an attempt to call the benevolent, presumed divine being, back to his adored place of veneration.

Some may have committed suicide in sheer grief. However, they shouldn't have been over-worried about the strange absence, for it was not long before the blessed Cube did return to them, and stated, quite plainly, that they were in danger from enemies that lived in the high mountains above.

The Cube itself, not being a physical being in any sense that can ever be imagined, was quite powerless to do anything to stop the coming conflagration. Or, at least it must have been contrary to its personal ethics or programming to do anything contrary, or interfere. A frightening display of its aerial prowess, and a few trumpet-like blasts of its thunderous voice, might have gone a long way toward calming the warlike passions of the enemy tribe.

It, of course, attempted nothing of the sort, but instead prepared the tribal people of the valley to face the coming onslaught. He taught them some finer arts of physical defense, encouraged them to sharpen their flint knives, prepare their stone axes, prepare thousands of torches, fashion bows and advanced spear tips, and generally did as much as possible to arm and ready a still primitive people for a battle the likes of which had never before been enacted upon the face of the world.

And why did such a mysterious, advanced being go to this alarming length, you might ask? Well, one possibility might be the far-reaching scope of the personal vision of whoever (or whatever) sent the Cube to begin with. We recently had occasion to glance at an article that suggested that all of man's great evolutionary leaps could be attributed to his willingness, not to live in peace, but to fester in a state of almost-permanent war. Truly, mankind has lived awash in a mighty ocean of blood and grue all the days of his existence of this revolving orb in the middle of space, and much of his technology and learning has, indeed, been a direct or indirect result of his striving toward better, faster, and more efficient methods of killing his fellow men in fierce and determined, and often pointless struggles.

C'est la Vie!

Of course, their preparations alone would make for an entire new book, and the resultant innovations in killing developed during this short period of preparation by the tribesman of the lower valley were considerable and would fascinate archaeologists or historians who happened upon this particular period (if this particular period actually existed in the way in which the boy's vision revealed). We have already demanded much of the reader, having taken him from the creeping hallways and somber farm fields of haunted Indiana to a place in the ancient past, back beyond the mists of recorded history, and we can be sympathetic at the possible stretching of credulity demanded of You, Dear Reader, and we do not mean to test your patience. Not in the least.

When the attack finally came, it was a slaughter the likes of which would sicken the most battle-hardened veteran of modern military conflicts. Men fell by spear and axe, heads were shattered by stones fired from slings, warriors were run through with sharpened stakes, and burned alive where they stood. Women and children fell prey to the shattering club, and volleys of arrows for the first time in history flew through the air like deadly, skinny insects, laying waste to waves of battling tribesmen, who ran down from the hills to die, and retreat, and come down in fury, in a berserker's rage of vengeance, once more.

The sandy earth grew sodden with blood, but the worst was the whirlwinds of flame, as crops and building and structures newly erected were torched by the enemy force. Likewise, the strongholds of the tribe from the hills were soon overrun and invaded by the people from the valley, who burned their homes and hovels and huts, and pillaged what little they had, in hatred and revenge.

Suddenly, the future chronicle of the human race was born in a torrent of blood and fire and pain, and the Cube, who was monitoring and recording all of this for later evaluation, remained curiously silent and aloof through it all. The vision, as far as the boy could see, began to fade, and pull back, until he realized he was staring at a series of moving images projected on an unfurled scroll. Holding the scroll, in long, skeletal, brown fingers, was the image of a being that was clearly not of this earth. The skin looked like wet clay; the head was enormous, while the arms and chest and neck were bony and thin. The mouth was a bare slit and the nose a slight indentation.

In the skinny fingers was held a series of scrolls. These images, these peculiar visions of a past that could be verified by no historian, played out upon the face of the scroll. Then, when a particular scene was finished, the scroll blew away into the darkness in which the being seemed to be standing. The scroll would then burst into flame.

There were many such scrolls, and the being seemed to speak in a voice that was rapid, mechanical, yet strangely smooth and comforting. The boy must have tossed and turned in the "sleep" of his strange vision, as future scenes that he would not even later remember were played out in front of his mind's eye.

One scene that did stick out starkly in his consciousness was an alien, burning world, and a picture of forests of trees ablaze.

On our world, the ground is on fire. But there are still trees.

He didn't understand what the being meant by that, but, like all the others, the scroll blew from the skinny tips of the being's fingers, and burst into a ball of flame.

Then, the final scroll, this time, floating in the darkness only momentarily before the boy emerged from his vision. This scroll bore a strange symbol upon it, like a hand with an eye in the center of the palm.

Suddenly, the boy emerged upward from unconsciousness, still feeling the heavy magnitude of what he had just experienced. He reeled from bed and went outside, into the cool stillness of the night.

Outside, he could see the star-strewn heavens and all the glory and majesty of them as they covered a mystery called life. He began to walk the silent streets. He knew not where he was headed.

It was only a short time later that the invasive, alien force that had seemed to creep, steadily, into the boy's mind, began to present itself in the form of strange "inner-dialogues," that he could sometimes speak, if he became relaxed enough. The general term applied to this sort of endeavor is often "channeling," but it is not an entirely satisfactory term, and it lacks a certain dignity today.

Mediumship, a form of communication as old as the Biblical story of the Witch of Endor (and really quite a bit older), is proscribed by all major religions, but still exists nonetheless in the form of various strains of spiritualism. The boy knew nothing, at the time, about spiritualism, but he and a strange group of friends that gathered around him would listen in rapt wonder to his trancing pronouncements, and the boy became very adept at laying back, losing himself, and letting his consciousness go. In time, another voice would begin to speak.

What it said was often inscrutable and cryptic, but it did, at times, relate information that the boy himself would have had no way of knowing had it not been by some supernatural means. At first, it had been helpful to employ a Ouija Board (a device that can be both useful and dangerous), but soon the small group that had gathered around the erstwhile prophet found they no longer needed the thing, and he could simply lay down before them, close his eyes, and begin to pronounce verily on any number of startling topics.

A small book resulted from this, a self-published book that was not very good, altogether. Later, the boy would attempt a volume of automatic writing that was little more than a few gems amid a lot of rubbish. Everything is a learning experience, we suppose.

At the risk of making this into an entirely different book, another epic altogether, we will relate one startling occurrence that happened, late one evening, in an attic room of an old building, while the boy was having a soiree of amused and nervous friends ask him (or rather "it") questions. Cryptic answers followed, but soon, another personality began to emerge, a much more hostile, alien personality that called itself "Robert."

"Robert," a not altogether friendly chap, cautioned them that they should seek out a "combination of red and white lights" and a "tire swing," of all such outlandish pairings, and then growled, moaned, and threw the boy into a near panic. One of his friends raced to turn on the lights, and it was soon decided that they should go driving out into the countryside in search of these cryptic clues.

Of course, it was a nerve-shattering pleasure to navigate the back roads of Indiana in search of geographic spots suggested by summoned spirits, but the boy was acutely aware of "Robert" still having a firm hold on at least some part of his consciousness.

They drove for what seemed an interminable amount of time, until finally passing a church. Suddenly, the boy felt a tug at his brain.

"There's something about that church. I think we should go back. Drive into the lot."

They had already driven well down a deserted road, past the church, but the driver, a large, gregarious young woman who was always up for a bit of mischief, decided that turning back must be the proper thing to do.

She found a dirt driveway, turned the car around, and proceeded back to the church. She drove onto the vacant blacktop, and the boy said, "Go back as far as you can."

Sure enough, the headlights of the car fell upon a single, solitary, barren

tree, from which a gnarled branch bore an old rope with a tire affixed to it.

"It could have just been a coincidence," the boy often thought to himself, later. But he didn't really believe that. No, it had simply been a small prank on the part of a very prankish discorporate personality, to prove the validity of what it said.

After all, what were the chances that he would be guided to that particular church, in which, out back, they had the exact same sort of swing the entity that spoke through him had mentioned?

Next, they drove until they found themselves near an airport. Looking up, he saw a row of street lights with a strange, red, beacon-like attachment on the end of each. Of course! The red and white light combination!

He pointed this out to his fellow passengers, and one of them, a rather naive young fellow in the back, expressed that he "was impressed, now."

He was, however, not impressed enough to keep along for the ride, and after dropping him back at his house, in the wee hours of the morning, the boy looked at the woman driving and asked, "Do you feel like going home yet?"

"No. Not particularly. Let's drive some more. C'mon, it's not that late."

Now, they headed out into the deep country, into the sticks. Past ramshackle farmhouses, cold fields encircled by rusty fences and rotten posts, and, everywhere, the dying fruits of the earth choked deeply with weeds. Beyond patches of such forlorn farmyard and forbidding field, were dark houses and drooping barns, dilapidated dwellings of those long dead and forgotten and reborn to new lives in other, more interesting times and placcs.

The sky was surprisingly dark, and the moon was waning into a phosphorescent scythe. There were few stars to boast of, and the roads gave off a feeling as curiously empty and dead as the feelings of subtle dread that had begun to accumulate in the car the farther out they drove and the earlier the morning grew.

"Do you want to go home, yet?"

"No, there's something more. Something to see. I can feel it."

They suddenly turned down a road between two tall, weed-choked fields. Suddenly, off to the side, sparkling in the air like a surrealistic jewel, the boy could see a slow-moving, brilliant object.

It floated slowly over the darkened ground below, making no sound. And it was lit like no aircraft ever to depart from the runway of the airports of this planet.

"And there it is. That's it."

The boy was suddenly terrified. The woman, whether in a heat of curiosity or sheer panic, actually floored the accelerator on the empty road, meaning, in a burst of bravery, to get as close to what-ever it was as possible.

The boy begged her to stop, knowing full-well that whatever they encountered could be dangerous, even deadly. At the very least, he reckoned in a moment of panic, it could threaten madness.

It was nearly above the road now, glowing like a ball of slow, silent white flame, and they would soon be directly beneath it, whatever it was. In front of them, the car headlights fell upon the presence of

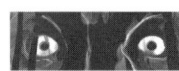

an old rusted railroad tracks, cutting through the adjoining fields. This necessitated slowing down, and so she brought he car to a more respectable speed. Suddenly, ahead of them, a pair of headlights instantly made themselves apparent. There was another vehicle coming toward them, from the direction where the thing was floating, now positioned almost directly over the country road.

The boy felt his breath suck inward.

It was a solid black van.

Dear Reader, I would like to tell you that both of those individuals found a way to turn their car around suddenly, move back down the road, and that the mysterious object and the black van followed them, along the highway, back to their common place of residence. I would like to be able to tell you that the van passed them up on the highway, speeding ahead, but that the object followed them (chased them really) back home, and that they stood out in the front yard and looked at it as it remained, stationary in the air, for what seemed like hours.

"It might be a satellite."

"It's too big and bright to be a satellite. I don't know what that thing is."

But it didn't move. It stayed in the air above the rooftops, sparkling like a miraculous, sky-borne diamond. They seemed to stand out, under an old tree in the front of the building, and watch the thing all night.

———————————

I would like to be able to tell you that this series of events is what transpired, and, as far as both of the witnesses remember, consciously, this is exactly what *did* transpire. But, if you have learned nothing else from reading this small volume of wonders, we would hope that, by now, you would realize that things aren't always what they seem, and life, as a dream remembered through a glass darkly, can often fool us into accepting that which we'd like to believe happened, or which we can logically account for, as compared to the hidden reality of our lives that exists, like a dawning realization at the tip of our conscious thoughts.

I am now not sure what happened to those two on that strange night, or if, indeed, anything happened at all. Or if something more strange and wonderful than we can imagine transpired, and, for some reason we do not or cannot understand, they have had their memories erased or suppressed.

I cannot say anything for certain. I cannot say that extraterrestrials do not exist. I cannot say that extraterrestrials do not abduct people, or that they do not fly in amazing ships that operate on principles of physics and technology that we cannot, as of yet, even begin to understand. As a matter of fact, I can't even begin to, definitely say, that there are extraterrestrials (as we properly understand the term) at all.

We live at the edge of a vast abyss, staring downward into limitless darkness, and the more we understand, or think we understand, the less we know. Where does fantasy end, and reality begin? What is the difference between history and folklore, between science and magic, between the paranormal, and the mundane? Are we the result of an intergalactic experiment, biological evolution, an angry, omnipotent God, or simply one consciousness experiencing itself in a variety of different forms (as is suggested by New Age guru and conspiracy theorist David Icke)? Is reality a cold, hard trip from cradle to grave, with nothing but eternal death beyond the final failings of the physical form? Or is reality an ever-shifting prism, a kaleidoscope of alternating realities and strange portals, dimensions to far-off places right around the corner, and strange mirror-image worlds that are not quite our own, but not quite another, either.

We cannot say anything for certain, at this point.

As for the boy, he went on to try and ply his strange talent for small audiences, but he later abandoned this. Why, specifically, he cannot say. Somehow, it seemed to become too exhausting, and after awhile the "channels" that communicated through him became dimmer and dimmer.

And I should know.

I was that boy.

Still am.

And now I bet you find yourself really amazed, don't you?

~Tom Baker
11/23/08

Bibliographic Essay

I have chosen to eschew the conventional bibliography in favor of simply lending you a hand as to what books and websites to pursue should you be interested in learning more about these subjects. And, of course, to credit what books and websites proved most valuable to me while completing this book.

The single most valuable book proved in and of itself to be *Hoosier Hauntings* by K.T. MacRorie, published by Thunder Bay Press of Michigan, in 1997. This book was an incredible, delicious potpourri of fascinating tales and folklore, such as the story of "Morning Glory" and "Culbertson Mansion," as well as many other anecdotes used in this book. I recommend this book most highly to anyone wanting a quick, entertaining read, and an excellent overview of the subject of paranormal phenomenon and ghost folklore in Indiana.

Of course, the excellent books of Mark Marimen (whom I have personally met) should never be missed by anyone interested in supernatural phenomenon in the Hoosier state. These include *Haunted Indiana and Haunted Indiana 2*, both of which were utilized while researching this book, and both of which are published by Thunder Bay Press of Michigan. *Haunted Indiana 2* was published in 1999.

It was from the book *Haunted Indiana 2* by Mr. Marimen, from which I gleaned the information about the haunted house on Boots Street in Marion, in the chapter *Jittery Jaunt*. Mr. Marimen's books should be de rigueur for any fan of this particular regional supernatural genre.

Hoosier Folk Legends by Ronald L. Baker, published by Indiana University Press of Bloomington in 1982, offered many, many useful anecdotes and stories, ranging from "butter witches" to UFOs that burn folks' clothing off. This book, which is academic and consists of a number of collected folkloric stories from "average folks," is nonetheless excellent and entertaining, and should be sought out and read greedily for the panoply of wonders within.

The Strange World of Frank Edwards, a collection of the paranormal writer's best pieces, edited by Rory Stuart, provided the story of "Lady Wonder," as well as the story of the "Dream that Captured a Killer." *The Strange World of Frank Edwards* was published by Lyle Stuart, Inc. of Secaucus, New Jersey in 1977. It is probably out of print, but anything by Frank Edwards is well worth tracking down.

Historic Haunted America by Michael Norman and Beth Scott, provided the story of the "Phantom Soldiers of Tippecanoe." This book, as well as the companion volumes such as *Haunted Heartland*, are incredible collections of stories from all around America. They are quite popular. *Historic Haunted America* was published by Tor Books of New York, in 1995.

Much of the material on Bigfoot and lake monsters was taken from *Strange Indiana Monsters* by Michael Newton, who seems to be a fount of comprehensive research on the subject of cryptozoology as it relates to the Hoosier state. The book is heavily documented and thorough, and the place to go if you are interested in monsters and unknown animals in Indiana.

Were it not for my strange discovery of the book *Telephone Between Worlds*, I would never have learned of the life of medium Richard Zenor, or that he was from Terre Haute. The book, by James Crenshaw, is still in print I believe (amazingly enough) but may be hard to obtain. It is a serious exploration of spiritualistic beliefs and philosophy, and author Crenshaw knew his subject well. The edition I have was published by Devorss and Co. of Los Angeles, in 1950.

Lesser sources in my bibliography include such books as *Intruders* by Budd Hopkins, a book about Mr. Hopkin's ongoing investigation of a UFO abduction case out of Indianapolis, *Communion* and *Confirmation*, both by Whitley Strieber (these titles are all well known) and *The Fellowship: Spiritual Contact Between Humans and Outer Space Beings* by Brad Steiger, published by Ivy Books of New York, in 1988. These books, most of which can be easily obtained, are invaluable to developing an understanding of the interaction between supernatural UFO beings, and human beings. Also, the ground-breaking work of French scientist Jacques Vallee, in books such as *Dimensions* (published by Contemporary Books of Chicago in 1988) and *Messengers of Deception: UFO Contacts and Cults* (currently published by Daily Grail publishing), offer an intense look at the UFO phenomenon from an occult perspective not often considered and not generally popular (but most probably correct, in this author's opinion). Mr. Vallee is comprehensive, examines the complete folklore of mysterious visitors from the sky, and best of all, served as the model for the French Ufologist in Stephen Spielberg's classic film *Close Encounter's of the Third Kind*. These books are both still in print, and readily available for order.

For an understanding of the "feral nature" of man, or, what turns some men into veritable "wolves," I relied upon maverick publisher, Adam Parfrey's excellent essay "Latter-Day Lycanthropy: Battling for the Feral Soul of Man," in his cult collection of sub cultural essays and provocations, *Apocalypse Culture*, published by his own Feral House imprint in 1988. Though I would recommend this book for anyone

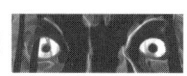

with a strong stomach and a stronger curiosity about the modern madness we all are forced to dwell in, I would strongly caution: This book is NOT for children.

By far, though, the most important author I feel anyone can read concerning the paranormal (besides the immortal Charles Fort) is none other than John Alva Keel, author of the popular book *The Mothman Prophecies* (a popular and readily-available book made into a movie with Richard Gere), and the exhaustive magnum opus *UFOs: Operation Trojan Horse,* an enormous study of the UFO phenomenon that goes from ancient history to modern contact, and offers a Unified Field Theory of the unexplained that, quite literally, may leave the reader gasping for air with every sentence and paragraph. Keel has stared the paranormal in the face, and lived to tell the tale, and is the best, most knowledgeable source of information and speculation and theory) that I have ever encountered. His books are frightening, too. Really frightening.

UFOs: Operation Trojan Horse has been published in a number of editions over the years (each with seeming variations on the original title), but should be easy to track down and order from the internet by those with the courage and commitment.

Other authors worth checking out, for a variety of reasons, include conspiracy theorist and New Age philosopher David Icke, who promotes an "inter-dimensional" view of reality as well as extraterrestrials and spirits, and Jerome Clark, who has written several popular compendiums of paranormal phenomenon and folklore. Mr. Clark's books are very popular, and Mr. Icke has a large popular website, although his books can be harder to find in "brick and mortar" shops.

We considered the inclusion of internet websites in this essay, but on further reflection, decided against it—we can only recommend the website of the Mutual UFO network of Indiana (http://indianamufon. homestead.com/), which was invaluable in learning of many of the aspects of the "Southern Indiana Wave."

Websites come and go, and they are rarely very thorough and can often not be trusted as sources. Also, any Google search will pull up dozens of them, of varying degrees of depth and accuracy.

And that, as they say, is a wrap.

Endnotes

1. Parfrey likewise gives us the account of a "performance artist" named "Kristine Ambrosia," whose act involved her being lowered into an oil drum while volunteers made tribal banging. She would then "transform" herself into a werewolf, and act the part to perfection, quite possibly scaring the hell out of whoever dared to show up and give her an audience.

2. One group of farmers apparently did make a brave (or foolhardy) attempt to track down Silas Shimmerhorn, journeying so far as to go to his "Bat Cave." All they apparently found were the remains of some rough bedding and a rusted old rifle bearing his initials.

3. It was claimed, by some Airship witnesses, that they could hear strangely beautiful music coming from the ships, and in one case, that of Alexander Hamilton in Kansas, that he could hear four "of the strangest creatures he ever saw" speaking in a foreign language in the cabin right above where he stood.

4. West Virginia's elusive, mysterious psychic sentinel "Mothman" is described, similarly, as having no head but having two burning red eyes in the center of its chest.

5. It is supposed that the Nazis, and Hitler himself, were ardently influenced by the occult, and there are even books (such as *The Nazis and the Occult* by Dusty Sklar, and *The Spear of Destiny* by Trevor Ravenscroft) that suggest that Hitler was after certain "occult items" and searching out lost treasures and the location of the fabled Atlantis. Indeed, much of Nazi imagery and philosophy is drawn, not only from Teutonic legend and lore, but from Theosophy, a religion founded by spirit-medium Helena Petrovna Blavatsky, who suggested that the roots of the "Aryan" race lay in Atlantis. Hitler, a student of the occult from his Vienna days, was a voracious reader of a magazine called *Ostara*, published by occultist Jorge Lans Von Liebenfchls, who can be linked to the mystical Thule Society and the pseudo-occult lodges operating at the time that combined pan-Aryan mysticism, nationalism, and spiritualism in a heady, bizarre mixture. Of course, any further speculation on this theme is, strictly-speaking, outside the humble scope of the present volume.

6. This phenomenon, often referred to as "Electronic Voice Phenomenon" or EVP is gaining in popularity, and an entire subculture exists of people who claim to communicate with spirits via the medium of recorded sound, either on cassette tape or, as is most often the case today, digital recorder and even radio signals and computer. Some quite startling examples of this phenomenon (which was pioneered by Dr. Konstantin Raudive in the late fifties) have been captured, and although frequently skeptics accuse the purported transmission of being nothing more than "interpreted gibberish" coming from chance sounds, or even stray signals from radio stations, this author has heard examples of EVPs that would chill your blood.

Of course, anyone with a recording device may try this for themselves by simply asking purported spirits questions and letting the tape or digital recorder run on at length, but remember: be patient. They don't, usually, come rushing in all at once to say "hello!" It can be a very tedious, long wait until results are obtained.

7. The contents of said letter, quoted in *Hoosier Folk Legends* by Ronald A. Baker, are as follows:

> *"Be welcome, fiery guest, but do not spread further; this I count thee as a penance in the name of God the Father, the Son, and the Holy Ghost.*
>
> *I command thee, fire, by the power of God, which does all and creates all, thou wilt stand still and not go farther as certain as Jesus stood on the Jordan when he was baptized by John the Saint.*
>
> *This I count thee, fire, as a penance, in the name of the Holy Trinity.*
>
> *I command thee, fire, by the Power of God, thou wilt allay these flames as certain as Maria retained her virginity alone of all women, as she kept herself so chaste and pure, so, therefore, fire cease thy fury.*
>
> *This I count thee, fire, as a penance in the name of the Most Holy Trinity.*
>
> *I command thee, fire, thou wilt smother thy heat, in the name of the dear blood of Jesus Christ, which He has shed for us, for our sins and crimes.*
>
> *This I count thee, fire, as penance, in the name of God the Father, the Son, and the Holy Ghost.*
>
> *Jesus Nazarenus, a King of the Jews, help us out of these dangers of fire and save this country and limits from all plague and pestilence."*